BEGINNER'S GUIDE TO
Garden Planning AND Design

50 Simple Gardening Ideas for Adding Style & Personality to Your Outdoor Space

CREATIVE
HOMEOWNER®

Helen Yoest

DEDICATION

For my three favorite flowers, Lara Rose, Lily Ana, and Michael Aster. Watching you grow and explore is the best part of my life—both in the garden and out.

CreativeHomeowner.com

Copyright © 2012, 2024 Helen Yoest and Creative Homeowner

Beginner's Guide to Garden Planning and Design (2024) is a revised and expanded edition of *Gardening with Confidence* (2012), self-published by Helen Yoest. Revisions include a new title and design and updated text and new photographs throughout.

Beginner's Guide to Garden Planning and Design
Managing Editor: Gretchen Bacon
Acquisitions Editor: Lauren Younker
Editor: Sherry Vitolo
Designer: Freire Disseny + Comunicació
Proofreader: Kelly Umenhofer
Indexer: Jay Kreider

ISBN 978-1-58011-608-4

Library of Congress Control Number: 2024930449

We are always looking for talented authors. To submit an idea, please send a brief inquiry to acquisitions@foxchapelpublishing.com.

Printed in China
First Printing

Creative Homeowner®, *www.creativehomeowner.com*, is an imprint of New Design Originals Corporation and distributed in North America by Fox Chapel Publishing Company, Inc., 800-457-9112, 903 Square Street, Mount Joy, PA 17552.

Unless otherwise noted, photography is by Helen Yoest. Photo on page 204 by Juli Leonard.

The following images are from Shutterstock.com: front cover, 32–33, 34–35: L. Feddes; back cover background, 202–203: Maria Evseyeva; back cover top, 42–43: Eric Krouse; back cover second from top, 10–11, 108–109: Molly Shannon; back cover third from top, 40–41: Steve Cymro; back cover bottom, 148–149: Scorpp; inside back cover: Yoko Design; 1, 4, 46–47: Zabavna; 8–9, 66–67: Hannamariah; 16–17: Toa55; 18–19: p-jitti; 20–21: Elena Elisseeva; 22–23: KELENY; 24–25: Shelli Jensen; 26–27: Douglas Barclay; 28–29: Theresa Lauria; 36–37, 38: Joe Kuis; 44–45: Gardens by Design; 48–49, 182: Paul Maguire; 50–51: Mikeal Broms; 52–53: romakoma; 54–55: fotocraft; 56–57: Jamie Hooper; 58–59: LENA GABRILOVICH; 60–61: T photography; 62–63: Hanahstocks; 64–65: Aleksandr Kondratov; 68–69: ifiStudio; 70–71: Matthew J Thomas; 72–73: Ginger Wang; 76: Art_Textures; 80–81, 134–135, 152–153: Jorge Salcedo; 84–85: Matthew Ashmore; 86–87: Sidneyphotos; 88–89: Worraket; 90–91: John Szpyrka; 92–93: Gillian Pullinger; 94–95: MagicMore; 96–97: nnattalli; 98–99: U__Photo; 100–101: Antonina Potapenko; 102–103: qingqing; 110–111: Rob Hainer; 112–113: Jason Finn; 116–117: MZinchenko; 118–119: Beekeepx; 120–121, 196–197: Kathryn Roach; 122–123, 150–151: 1000 Words; 128–129: nieriss; 130–131: New Africa; 132–133: Bartkowski; 136–137: PRILL; 140–141: Chen Liang-Dao; 142: funkyteddy; 144–145: JohnnyZMI; 146–147: pim pic; 154–155:friedgreenbeans; 156–157: Vilda.S; 158: sirtravelalot; 160–161: AngieC333; 162–163: Maximiliane Wagner; 164—165: Andrii Salomatin; 166–167: Baloncici; 168–169: Cynthia Shirk; 170: James Laurie; 172–173: Ms.Karyn; 174–175: Leena Robinson; 176–177: Susan Law Cain; 178: Martins Vanags; 180–181: Alex Manders; 184–185: Konmac; 187: Debu55y; 188–189: symbiot; 190–191: Delpixel; 198–199: Orhan Cam; 200–201: Pefkos

FOREWORD

It is always a joy to learn new things and to be reminded again of others. I'm always looking for resources to continue to hone my gardening design skills. *Beginner's Guide to Garden Planning and Design* accomplishes just that. This book methodically outlines a foundation of best practices starting with the basics and adding to those building blocks to help us develop into the best gardeners that we can be. The confidence gained from understanding how to add design features, while developing our own personal style, will take us and our gardens to that next level.

Beginner's Guide to Garden Planning and Design is a true labor of Helen Yoest's love of our common pursuit. Helen has outlined 50 ways to add style to express one's personal creativity in the garden when in fact her 50 will inspire at least 50 more ideas in us.

Helen covers all of the topics that any beginning gardener will want to know about and offers more seasoned gardeners many inspiring ideas. I am taken in by all the themes but particularly by the chapters on garden planning and creating your garden environment. I am crazy about moss gardening and all the wildlife topics she documents in the book.

In this book, she instills gardening self-assurance with her relaxed and easy, unprescribed approach. She introduces us to basic concepts and patiently explains them with an informative and gentle voice written with the ease of someone who has garnered a wealth of personal experience over the years—making her an ideal guide to lead readers through all the helpful ideas and concepts. She gives readers the courage, the confidence, and the tools to strike out on their own and develop their personal style. Each step is a rewarding journey encouraging us to take that next step, then another and yet another.

Beginner's Guide to Garden Planning and Design provides all of us an overview of garden style without dictating what it *should* be. Helen helps readers explore, discover, and express what their own style actually is. She leads us through this voyage of self-expression not as a designer would approach the subject, but as an enlightened guide who over the years has worked through the obstacles. It's obvious Helen has practiced and discovered what works and what doesn't.

This experience helps her to communicate on the same level as the reader. Like working through a puzzle with a trusted friend, she gives us the gift of gardening success through self-realization.

P. ALLEN SMITH

CONTENTS

INTRODUCTION

Each of us brings a unique quality to everything we do. While garden types are definable—cottage, formal, contemporary—your personal style will make your garden unique. There are some gardens that make me feel like I'm in the pit of a well-balanced orchestra, with each instrument—a flower, a shrub, a tree—insignificant on its own but lyrical within the arrangement. These gardens may not all be expensive, but they are all thoughtfully arranged, with each addition carefully considered. The rhythm, the scale, the color echo—it all works well together. Nothing dominates or upstages the other important performers.

Considering the garden as a whole allows it to sing. Knowing what makes a garden work begins with understanding the elements of a garden. Once you understand how to use and place elements, an arbor, a trellis, a bench, you can give your garden a voice.

This book is designed to give you insight into the basics of arranging the components of your garden. The confidence you'll gain from knowing how to add design features, while developing your own personal style, will help take your garden to the same levels occupied by the fantastic gardens that inspired you to begin your own work of art in the first place.

The gardens with the most melodic voices are those that reflect good design along with the owner's individuality. You may find you're comfortable with your fashion or interior style, but once you step outside, you lack the confidence to create a beautiful space. The purpose of this book is to teach you how to develop a stunning design that reveals your own signature.

Keep in mind that each childhood memory, each turn of the page in a gardening book or magazine, and every trip to a botanical garden has influenced your gardening style. It's not a mystery. Hand me a garden magazine you've just read, and I can tell your garden style by reading the dog-eared pages. If you peek at the colors in your bedroom closet, you'll realize they're echoed in the garden; racks of red or pink or blue or yellow clothing often repeat as rows of colorful flowers or foliage in your garden beds. Even the way you hang your family photos on the refrigerator door can say a lot about your gardening style. Those of you who allow your photos to touch and overlap or to be a bit off-kilter will gravitate to a certain gardening style. Those of you who don't want your photos to touch at all will likely incline toward a different style.

If you express your true self and let your passion be your guide, your unique style will always be the right choice.

Natural curiosity and wanderlust took me around the world several times over, and with each trip, I sought out great gardens along the way. I learned to appreciate each and every garden type and all the many styles that fit within each. I've never met a garden I didn't like. It's true. From frothy cottage styles to minimalist, contemporary styles. I see something to appreciate in each garden I visit.

During my career working for of some of the nation's leading shelter magazines and gardening organizations, I found myself in a position to evaluate gardens for touring and publication merit. In every case, whether I saw them for a tour or a magazine, the most memorable gardens had good design, with the homeowner's unique touch.

This book shares my design perspective, providing tips that you can apply to your garden at home. Each chapter will walk you through an element of design, allowing you to think about your own situation at home. Then you can add your own flair so that you can create a fantastic garden, a garden that sings.

So, get comfy and come along with me as we journey down the garden path.

HELEN YOEST

Flowers are just one of the tools for adding
color and uniqueness to a garden.

CARVING OUT SPACE

Nature has a magic number: 3. Threes abound in all forms of art, nature included. It's called the "rule of thirds." Used in architecture, painting, photography, and landscape design, the rule of thirds helps put things into perspective. It's the handiest tool to use whenever you want to create art, and landscape and garden design is certainly art.

When in doubt, break your design into thirds relative to a reference point. Most often that object will be the house itself. For example, you can use the rule of thirds when determining the width of front yard foundation beds (the plants that hug the house). Imagine if the front of the house were to lie down flat. The width of your foundation bed should be two-thirds of this length.

During new home construction, a row of foundation plants may be planted with no regard to the scale of the home. A single-story house might get the same depth of bed as a two-story house. A well-planned foundation bed, however, should be in proportion to the height of the house. With the bed done, you can then move on to your planting scheme.

Avoid putting all your planting beds around the perimeter of your house and the outer perimeter of the property line. It's easy to carve out creative space in other areas of your landscape, too.

When carving out space, it's important to know your "aspect"—basically, you need to know which way is north. It matters. Knowing your aspect will help you

This patio with steps and green areas creates a sense of balance within a smaller area.

understand the amount of sun the plants will receive. When you are locating features like patios, playsets, or swimming pools, you need to consider what sort of sun they'll get. South-facing slopes are hot and sunny. This would be a good location for a pool but not necessarily for a playset. Make sure that the place you've chosen for your sunny wildlife garden doesn't have too much shade.

Don't be afraid to use straight lines when forming bed edges, lawn shape, paths, and retaining walls. It is often best to mimic the shape of the house. Most home shapes have straight lines, and it works well to repeat this pattern. As you move away from the house, the lines can begin to form a more natural curve.

What do you like about the garden on pages 8–9? Most likely, it's not the plants or the accents that please you, although they

may. Take a closer look at the scale. Does it seem like it's a good fit? Creating a garden that is in scale with the lot and the house is one of the most important things you should consider for your design. This particular garden followed the rule of thirds with the patio, steps and landing, and privacy wall and gate beyond. It all works together beautifully.

For my home garden, I carved out space by using low boxwood hedges to define the edges. The straight lines give shape to the garden, allowing for year-round structure as the spring, summer, and fall flowers fade. Rows of trees can also give the same effect but with a more casual look.

Look at your existing beds. Are they pleasing in scale? If not, follow the rule of thirds, and increase or decrease your garden and its components to fill two-thirds the width of the closest structure, whether that structure is a house, fence, or gazebo.

Scale and Balance

When I first pulled up to the curb of our current home, it was obvious something was off. The two-story brick traditional home sat elevated about 8 feet (2.4m) higher than the sight line from the street. There were no large trees; the ground was covered in English ivy; and the foundation plantings were tight against the house, lined with identical boxwood hedges. To make matters worse, the faux Georgian-style home had these ostentatious columns that made the house look even more imposing from up high on its hill and entirely out of scale with everything surrounding it.

The first thing I did was extend the foundation beds out from the house to two-thirds the height of the house. Immediately, the house "felt" better, with the extended beds keeping the space from feeling tight and anxious. Even without plantings, widening the beds to be in scale with the house improved the look.

I also added trees to visually "bring down" the imposing height. The trees reached about two-thirds the height of the house. It worked. Today, the curbside view is of a home that is comfortably in scale with its surroundings.

This patio space is well-defined by the chairs and potted plants.

SKETCH YOUR IDEA

A garden is a place of wishes and wants. Often you imagine how something would look over in the corner or under the old oak tree. You wonder how a swing would look in that space. Or maybe you have a vision of a bench, plantings, or a container or two.

When planning your ideal garden, landscape designs are a valuable tool for placing plants, but you may decide to add much more than greenery or flowers. If you're considering creating a structure or putting "hardscaping" (paved areas, patios, or walkways) in an existing location, it's fun and easy to mark up your ideas on a photograph.

Confidence is born with pen and paper. Start by taking photos of your garden from various angles. With several copies of a photograph, printed from your computer or scanned, begin to play with lines, seating, buildings, arbors, and so on. Something as simple as marking over an existing bed can bring life to the image, allowing you to better visualize your thoughts. This technique is an amazingly handy way to look at your garden and imagine change, and it is used by many experienced landscape designers, including myself, to help homeowners visualize their new gardens.

When I planned my garden, I needed to keep my children in mind. Their time at home would be about half the time

This is the sketch I made over the "before" garden space.

I expected to live in the house, so my design needed to be adaptable. Using black-and-white printed copies of an overall view of my garden, I could mark up the photographs to see how my ideas would affect the space.

A long, flat area in the back garden serves as the kids' soccer field, where all sorts of balls are hit and kicked about. At one end of this space is a gazebo, and at the other end the children's playset. While the kids already enjoyed this area as their space, I planned how to add a bit of space here for myself, as well.

My dream came to life on the page as I sketched and crumpled one page after another until I got my thoughts down. I wanted to have a garden house. By sketching the garden house on the page, I could immediately see the scale I needed and the best position to place my new "home away from home." I was able to perfect the idea with my sketches. Today, the garden house sits in that area and brings many hours of enjoyment, whether I am alone or watching the kids play in the yard.

Before I did my sketch, I measured out a footprint of the space available for my garden house. What I could support with regards to space based on the footprint was at least 50 percent bigger than what the space could visually hold. The scale would have been overpowering. If I had put in a garden house based solely on the available space, I would have made a very big and expensive mistake. A simple sketch gave me perspective—I could *see* that my garden house would need to be smaller. This gave me a more informed point from which to move forward.

When sketching over printed photographs, I recommend using a permanent marker like a Sharpie® because the bold lines show up better on the page. Mark up your ideas on the printed photo. You don't even have to be good at drawing. (I'm certainly not.) Once the thick line is drawn, the existing lines fade away. Your new vision becomes clear and prominent. Immediately see the effect of widening the beds, changing the curve, or adding a bench, an arbor, or a gate. If you don't like what you see, crumple up the page and toss it into the recycling bin. Begin again. It's that simple.

One of the best advantages of this technique is that it allows you to see the scale at a glance. Even though you may not know the exact dimensions of your space, you'll have a relative sense of the proportions. Try it. You may just surprise yourself!

With your sketch, you can shop for your needs with a better understanding of what you have to work with. Take it with you when you shop at the garden store. Showing the staff your sketch will help them put the dimensions into perspective, too.

GARDENING WITH CONFIDENCE

Sketch First

After 25+ years in my garden, I began to evolve further. I started to move away from squiggles and curves in my front garden. My house was very linear, and I started to think that, rather than trying to mimic nature in a clearly manmade garden, it would be more appropriate to follow those lines.

I had trouble visualizing what the new bed lines would look like going from curved to straight. And I couldn't grasp how much this change would add to (or take away from) the current bed space. Within minutes, I'd printed photos of the front beds, pulled out a marker, and sketched on top of the pictures until I finally got it right. I could easily see on the paper where and how to change the existing lines into new edges. With this confidence, I took a can of blue marking paint and marked my new lines. I stood back, looked everything over, and said, "Yeah, man; that's it!" Now I can say that it's hip to be square.

The "after" photo of how my sketch became reality to transform my garden space.

PREPARE A PLAN

The best part of having a master plan to work from is that the design will carry you through the process of building your garden as resources become available. Not all the work needs to be done at once. Creating a plan, by yourself or with a designer, ensures that you are building a garden you'll love that will truly reflect your style and your vision.

Planning ahead also helps to minimize disruption to the garden—less will need to be edited, moved, or unearthed if, for example, you decide at a later date to add electric lines for night lighting. You will consider the obvious things, of course: your own preferences. Do you want a formal garden? A low-maintenance one? Wild splashes of color or orderly, precise patterns?

Consider the practical issues, too, like shade, sunlight, and soil type. When you're digging during the initial installation, it's the perfect time to add hardscape features and maybe an irrigation system. This will save your garden from being torn up as you move forward.

Reading the dog-eared pages of magazines you've saved is one of the best ways to quickly identify your gardening style. It's like reading palms or tea leaves—you'll find messages in the pages. Notice how each page reveals a pattern—perhaps you repeatedly gravitate to hot pops of red and purple. Perhaps you bent the corner of every page displaying a jumbled mix of plants, or maybe you leaned toward images filled with specimen plants—those

Garden plan sketches should include as much detail as possible, but still allow for flexibility.

LAYOUT PL

noteworthy enough to stand on their own. Identifying these themes will help you plan your garden.

If you feel that the whole process of creating the garden is overwhelming and daunting, help is but a conversation away. It might be as simple as asking a friend who has designed their own garden. Searching the internet is another good way to find designs you like. Many homeowners tinkering with their own designs who want to do their own work still rely on various professionals to help with certain steps along the way. Before you do your own final design, you may want to talk with a design professional. Hiring a landscape designer can be your best outdoor investment.

As an avid gardener and design professional, I understand how important getting another opinion can be. Long ago,

I left my ego at the curb, gaining the confidence to ask for help. Sometimes we just need to step away from something that is too familiar and ask for help. Decisions about a design element that could paralyze me in my own garden were the same decisions I could easily make for my clients.

A designer can help with patios, decks, and dining areas, or even with siting children's playsets. Designers can help you consider and place shade structures, rain gardens, a pool, or a spa. The placement of these elements within the design will give you a coherent plan for your entire lot, saving you from later heartache.

A designer can help you consider your future needs. Even if your budget doesn't currently fit your wish list, adding a future dream to your master plan will allow the garden to grow when your budget is ready.

GARDENING WITH CONFIDENCE

Be Practical

In 1997, when I first planned my current garden, I did it with kids in mind. At least, I thought I did. At the time, I had one child, who was one year old. Understanding what I needed for a child-friendly design was about as foreign to me as the Gettysburg Address would be to my dog, Pepper. You can read and do, plan and prepare; but life always happens. When planning your garden, be practical. Don't plant bee-enticing flowers along the entranceway, spilling into the path. Don't put pretty poisonous berries in direct reach of a curious toddler. Don't forget to include an area of lawn for spread-blanket picnics and daisy-chain making, cloud watching and counting shooting stars. Kids should feel their bare feet on cool summer grass and know the sensation of the blades tickling their toes. Your weekend doesn't have to be spent caring for a large expanse of lawn, but a patch of green can become a magical place where children build memories to last a lifetime.

Having a plan in place will help you visualize your new space even while it's still in progress.

As with most professionals, each designer gravitates toward a niche. Working with a designer who has a strong interest in horticulture will help you with the selection and care of your garden plants. Certainly, if you are looking for a professional to help choose plants to complete a design, a horticulturist is the one to call. Working with a designer who specializes in swimming pool garden design will enhance your plan if your focus is to add a pool.

When I added steps leading up an incline and through my mixed border, in an area that would also be a very visible focal point, I went to a professional who specialized in this kind of design. It was the best decision I ever made for my own design, and I don't say that lightly. I waited ten years to have the budget and inclination to make it happen.

Before your first visit with a landscape designer, make a list of all your wishes and wants. Identify any problem areas you want to address. Be sure to take your collection of dog-eared magazines along to show the designer your favorite garden elements and discuss why you are attracted to them.

It's fun going plant shopping and coming home to find the best place to plant your newest acquisition. You walk the garden, plant in both arms, resting it on your belly, until you find the perfect spot. It may not be the most practical thing you and I do, but we all do it. We will all continue to do it, so we might as well plan for it.

With a plan prepared, you can better understand where new plants will fit in the overall scheme of your gardening vision. If nothing else, you can more quickly find a home for any new addition.

VIEW FROM THE INSIDE

There's no reason to enjoy the garden only while outside. Most of us will spend more time inside than out, even those of us who spend a considerable amount of time in the garden. It is also true that not all family members will share your enthusiasm for being in the garden. However, they can be captivated when the view becomes a part of their everyday scenery. Concentrate on views in areas where you spend the most time, and your garden will be enjoyed by everyone all year long. In addition to designing your view from the inside, considering good placement of plantings can also provide other benefits, such as buffering a direct view from a neighbor's window or blocking the glare of the setting summer sun.

Whether by design or desire, the kitchen is the heart of a home. As the central hub, the kitchen is the gathering place to share a meal, do homework, work on a puzzle, or to slow down just a bit for conversation or silence. Why not admire the garden view, breathe in the fragrance, and perhaps even watch the wildlife that the garden attracts? Having the garden in view brings joy and conversation, from a quick walk through the kitchen to a long, lingering meal with friends and family around the kitchen table. You will never tire of the ever-changing scenery a window view provides. The addition of feeders will attract more birds and create the opportunity to watch them alight for a bite while you dine or clean up after a meal. Slow smiles will form on the faces of children and adults alike as

Your view of the garden through the window is just as important as the overall garden design.

they watch a cardinal take a sunflower seed and pause for a moment to see if the seed's weight is worthy of cracking.

Each window can frame a view to be enjoyed from inside. The living room window can frame a fountain birdbath as you sit on the couch to read. A casual look up from the book in your hand will bring the garden indoors for a moment as you reflect. Your thoughts may drift as you listen to the soothing sound of water or watch a bird sip and then fly away.

The dining room windows can hold scenes from your garden illuminated at night when the room is used most often. The light can fill the room for added romance and mystique while you enchant your guests. Outside lighting can add layers inside a room to create ambiance for your evening meals.

The view from the family room windows can fill the scene with the bright beauty of fragrant flowers, and when the windows are open, the scent will waft into the room. Add flowers with colors to match your interior décor to blend the rooms with the exterior spaces, visually expanding the interior space.

GARDENING WITH CONFIDENCE

Natural Entertainment

During the winter months, we add various bird feeders to a post outside the kitchen window where my family can view them during meals. We keep a field guide handy so the kids can easily identify the birds that come to visit the feeders. Often the squirrels will come as well, causing the kids to roar (mimicking their mother). We have tried various tactics to keep the squirrels away, with limited success. Our greatest victory comes from spreading out seed refilling. We found that this breaks the cycle, perhaps confusing the squirrels' routines for a while, and they seem to lose interest. Now, we fill the feeders on Saturday mornings and let the food last until the feeder needs refilling. Come the next Saturday, we refill. This way, we get to enjoy the birds while we are home to enjoy them. During the time no feed is in the feeder, the birds (and squirrels) go elsewhere in the garden to find food and, hopefully, dine on pesky insects.

A peek out into your garden creates a beautiful natural backdrop for indoor activities, too.

We can take our cue from Miss Elizabeth Lawrence (1904–1985), who was the first woman to earn a degree in landscape architecture from present-day North Carolina State University (1932) and later moved to Charlotte to write the garden column for the *Charlotte Observer*. Miss Lawrence wrote over 700 columns and several books from her home office overlooking her garden. With her typewriter arranged to provide a view of the garden—a garden designed with vanguard plants, a reflecting pond, paths, and a simple cinder-block wall—Miss Lawrence corralled all her garden loves and interests within view so that she never missed a moment in her garden as she went about her daily writing.

The outside view should also be an allure, a seduction to beckon you to come outside to interact with the garden. The view should call for you to come outside and bring a hot cup of tea or glass of wine to unwind at the end of a hectic workday. On days when the weather is frightful, the inside view will keep you in touch with nature and the rhythm of life that your garden provides.

RHYTHM, SCALE, AND BALANCE

When a garden scene takes your breath away, it's often hard to immediately identify why. If you look closer, something might pop out at you, revealing itself like a 3-D image. When that happens, the view in front of you most likely has good rhythm, appropriate scale, and is pleasingly balanced. Although it's difficult to explain in words, you know it when you see it—a birdhouse near a birdbath or a pattern of various perennials and shrub heights that pleases the eye.

In design, rhythm refers to the illusion of motion created through the arrangement of landscape elements. If done correctly, a landscape design leads the viewer's eye through the perspective, beyond the foreground to a more distant part of the landscape. If you wander down a well-designed garden path, the rhythm of the garden's elements will lead you where you want to go. When I redesigned my mixed border in my garden, I paid special attention to the rhythm and balance (see more on balance on pages 26–27) of the plants I added. I didn't want to look out at a wall of plants of equal sizes and weights. I wanted the space to have rhythm, a feeling as if one was lightly floating along and through the garden beds—gently weaving with a comfortable rhythm from one end to the other.

Scale is another crucial landscape element, and it serves to help the rhythm along. My rhythm would be off if my scale were wrong. Consider it in the context of interior design: a petite table would not be in scale with a massive couch. Similarly, a towering Southern magnolia

Mixing plant heights, types, and colors creates a sense of scale.

(*Magnolia grandiflora*) planted at the corner of a single-story ranch home would dwarf the structure and create an uncomfortable feeling.

Balance in design is about equality. It is achieved when elements are carefully arranged to produce the same visual weight on both sides of a central point. Let's consider the differences between symmetrical and asymmetrical balance.

Symmetrical balance is where the elements of design are equally divided. Most often this is the type of balance found in formal landscapes. A beautiful home with a central door and an equal amount of windows on each side, with a walkway leading through the middle of the front yard to the front door, is symmetrical. In such a design, plantings are typically placed to be mirror images, like the house itself, giving a feeling of stability and order.

Asymmetrical balance comes into play when working with structures that are not symmetrical. Asymmetrical gardens are usually more naturalistic and relaxed. The structure you may be working around might have the door off to the side, with the wall on one side taller or wider than the other. In these cases, it's often suggested to add a tree on the opposite side to mimic the height of the taller or wider wall.

Both balances are right for what they do. It is a matter of personal preference which type of balance your design sensibilities naturally gravitate toward.

Trellises and an armillary sphere help define a rhythm in what could be a chaos of abundant plants.

GARDENING WITH CONFIDENCE

Work Your Style into the Space You Have

Even when we know what sort of balance suits us, it's not necessarily what we have to work with.

My home is a two-story brick faux-Georgian. This was not at all my desired design, but it's my home, nonetheless. To make matters worse, there are massive, imposing columns across the front, and the house sits high on a slope. It has a strong character, almost demanding a certain style of landscape. When I first started working with the design, I actually accentuated the things I liked least about the house. I made it more formal because I thought I needed to be true to the house's style. Although I have often found myself in formal, symmetrical places and been very comfortable, I don't personally care for this type of design; I find it to be too stuffy. It was up to me to incorporate my style into the home's rigid symmetry and create a design that was less formal while still complementing the house.

At first it seemed like a tall order, but in the end, the plantings (and paint choices) toned down the stronger aspects of formality. I used two deciduous trees as vertical foundation plantings on either side of the centered front door. I wanted to take advantage of the west-facing sun's warming light in the winter while still providing shade against summer heat. The height of these trees added a welcoming transition between the imposing roofline of the house and the ground plantings. I also added a mixture of plants to the foundation beds, which lowered the towering scale of the house. Neither side looks alike. But the scale against the house is right, the balance on each side is equal, and seasonal plantings add rhythm to the design.

As you add accents to your existing garden bed, remembering these key elements will help you enhance your garden's beauty. Keep the size and visual weight of an accent proportionate to the bed plantings. A 10-foot-tall (3-m-tall) statue or birdhouse, for example, could overwhelm a bed where the tallest plant only measures 2 feet (61cm). Add plants that will ground your accent pieces and create rhythm and balance within the bed so that the accents comfortably blend in.

Take heart if you did not get a house that exactly matches your own design sensibilities. It shouldn't stop you from creating a garden that does!

CURB APPEAL

You don't have a second chance to make a good first impression. That old adage is as true for gardens as it is for people. It's especially true when it comes to curb appeal. Whether you want them to or not, most people will make snap decisions about you and your home based on your front yard. With just a little consideration, your front garden can go beyond simple appeal and actually welcome visitors and passersby, while at the same time letting them catch a glimpse of your personality.

What is your home's overall style? Does everything seem to fit? Begin assessing your home's curb appeal by starting at the edge of your property. Then walk up your drive or path and consider what others see. Can your visitor clearly find the front door? Is the front of the home pleasing to the eye year-round? With a fresh eye, evaluate what you see and think about where this may lead you. Look for spaces where you can add touches that speak to who you are while at the same time complementing your home.

Your best investment of time and money is focusing on the entryway. A visitor should not be confused—make the entrance clear and obvious. Ideally, the path should be wide enough for two adults to walk side-by-side (4 to 5 feet [1.2 to 1.5 m] across) and made with materials that complement your home's style. If you inherited the builder's standard 3-feet-wide (91.4cm-wide) concrete walkway, think about enhancing what you have by adding an

This entrance walkway garden with stone edging creates an immediate sense of welcome.

edge made from a complementary material, such as brick, or making room in your budget to work a new front walk into your landscape plan.

To improve your entryway, consider replacing existing hardware and light fixtures. For instance, if your home has rustic cottage charm, shiny brass accents may seem out of place. Instead, use oiled bronze; this popular choice will complement this style nicely. Change out all the hardware at the same time, including the lockset, kick plate, house numbers, and overhead light fixtures, to keep your theme consistent, all the time keeping everything within your chosen style.

Adding color at the entrance gives the most impact for welcoming visitors, and permanent color, such as those found in the door or shutters, can be easy to maintain. With just a little paint, your front door can go from boring to bold. Do you love the look of a red front door? Why not try purple, bright green, or canary yellow?

Add more color with plantings in containers and garden beds and also with garden accents. Container gardens at the entrance work well with any home style, and it's easy to experiment with their placement and arrangement. A staggered, asymmetrical placement with small groupings that get bigger as you approach the house leads the eye forward. Using colorful pots can add pizzazz, particularly when planted with flowers in complementary colors.

Whether you are accentuating a traditional, relaxed, or formal look, be sure to maintain that chosen look. Highly decorative pedestal urns will look out of place in the front garden of a contemporary-style home. Likewise, mirrored planters will not work well for a cottage-style home. A pair of pots can frame a front door with formality. For a more relaxed style, add layers of planters beyond the front steps. Finishing touches like hanging baskets from the roof eaves, placing flowers in window boxes, or adding arrangements on the porch will work with many home styles to leave an impact on visitors.

Just because you are working within your home's style, it doesn't mean you can't inject some of your own personality when you are refining your home's curb appeal. Garden art, boulders, or a bench can express your uniqueness. I have a fountain in my entryway that runs most months of the year. Accent lighting in trees or on the house and walkways can add some personality to your house at night, too, and possibly create a different vibe for evening visitors.

Well-maintained garden beds and borders are a must for good curb appeal. Keep your beds weeded, pruned, and top-dressed with fresh mulch. It doesn't matter how complementary the plants in your front garden are to your home or what color your front door is if the grounds aren't kept up well.

Go with your instincts when choosing the colors, the style of pots, the design of accent pieces, and the arrangement of lighting. With just a little attention to these details, you can begin creating curb appeal that reflects your personality, even before you open the door and say, "Welcome."

This red walkway adds color and personality to the entranceway.

GARDENING WITH CONFIDENCE

Be Bold

Too many homeowners play it safe when adding curb appeal. Why not express who you are as a gardener? If you love the color orange, paint your door orange. When my daughter was 11 years old, she did a survey of door colors (informal at best) and announced that the three most popular colors were brown, black, and white. How utterly boring! Mind you, my door is brown—but there are chartreuse accents that pop against the brown to bring happy, vivid color to all who enter. A small swatch of color can speak volumes about your vibrant personality. And remember, it's only paint. If you don't like it, it's easy to change again. (If applicable, consult with your homeowner association before changing colors on your home. There may be neighborhood rules to follow.)

STYLE

When I travel to see a garden, what's likely to make that garden pleasurable and memorable is when the homeowner has put their special imprint on it and displays a style that is unique. It's your garden, after all, so express yourself. While it's important to understand some design elements, such as those found in this book, putting your personal stamp on your garden is what will make it grand.

Often when I'm visiting gardens, it's not uncommon for homeowners to share with me a magazine feature that inspired them to design their gardens the way they did. Inspiration abounds—magazines, books, nature, or perhaps a neighbor. You simply add your own personal touches to make an idea your own. Wouldn't it be boring if all our gardens looked alike?

You may gravitate toward informal, naturalistic, or cute cottage styles, where the plants are free to roam and spill and touch, creating their own design. Or you may lean toward formal looks with pruned plantings and plants confined in their own space, no touching allowed. There is no right or wrong; it's only wrong if you plan something that isn't right for you. Your life experience will mold your design aesthetic.

Travel was (and still is) the single biggest influence in my design aesthetic. As with being well-read, being well-traveled opens one's eyes to many different experiences. And I liked them all. My challenge was to decide which experiences would influence me most.

Choosing the colors of your plants is a big part of garden design and style.

33

All the places I've traveled have helped me create my own personal style.

When my garden is written about, I often read words like "electric" and "eccentric," words used when something can't be described. If asked, I would tell you my garden is "cottage." That is basically how I identify my gardening style.

Even though cottage garden style lends itself to more additions, it's by no means a license for a free-for-all. It's best not to mix styles. You should try to keep your style

managed. Too many urns or benches, or themed gardens, can look pretentious and overdone.

If what you have isn't working, resist the urge to add more. It's probably more appropriate to edit than to add. I rely on advice attributed in various forms to Coco Chanel: "When accessorizing, always take off the last item you put on." It works in the garden, too. One winter, I realized I'd gone overboard with garden accents and art. I ended up removing all my garden accents and placing them in the middle of the backyard. One by one, I evaluated each piece on its merits. I only placed it back

This watering can and the various pots show the beauty of the in-process garden.

GARDENING WITH CONFIDENCE

Experiment with Your Style

There is a local woman whom I've not met, but I've been watching her build a garden. Each day, I drive by on my way here and there, and I delight in the personal touches she is adding to the space out front. I imagine what the space in the back must be like since people are more likely to put a restrained face on public view. If this is restrained, what magic must the back garden hold? I applaud her efforts.

Would I want what she has? Not necessarily, not from the perspective of design. But I'm envious of her willingness to experiment with her own personal style. I would be even more envious if I had remained reserved in my creativity, worrying about what others thought of my garden. I'm over that. I garden for my personal pleasure, to bring in the wildlife, and to share with the garden community my own personal style.

in the garden if it worked with the overall design. In the end, I saw my error and made it right—or at least, right for me. My garden has never looked better. After I finished, I realized the things I removed were of competing styles. What I kept all worked well together.

As long as you are true to your core style, your garden will blend together with a unified style rather than a mishmash. Decide on a style and build from there. If you want to be safe in your garden design, stay true to your personal style.

Be who you want to be in your garden. It's yours to do with as you please—within the constraints of homeowner associations and housemates.

CHAPTER

8

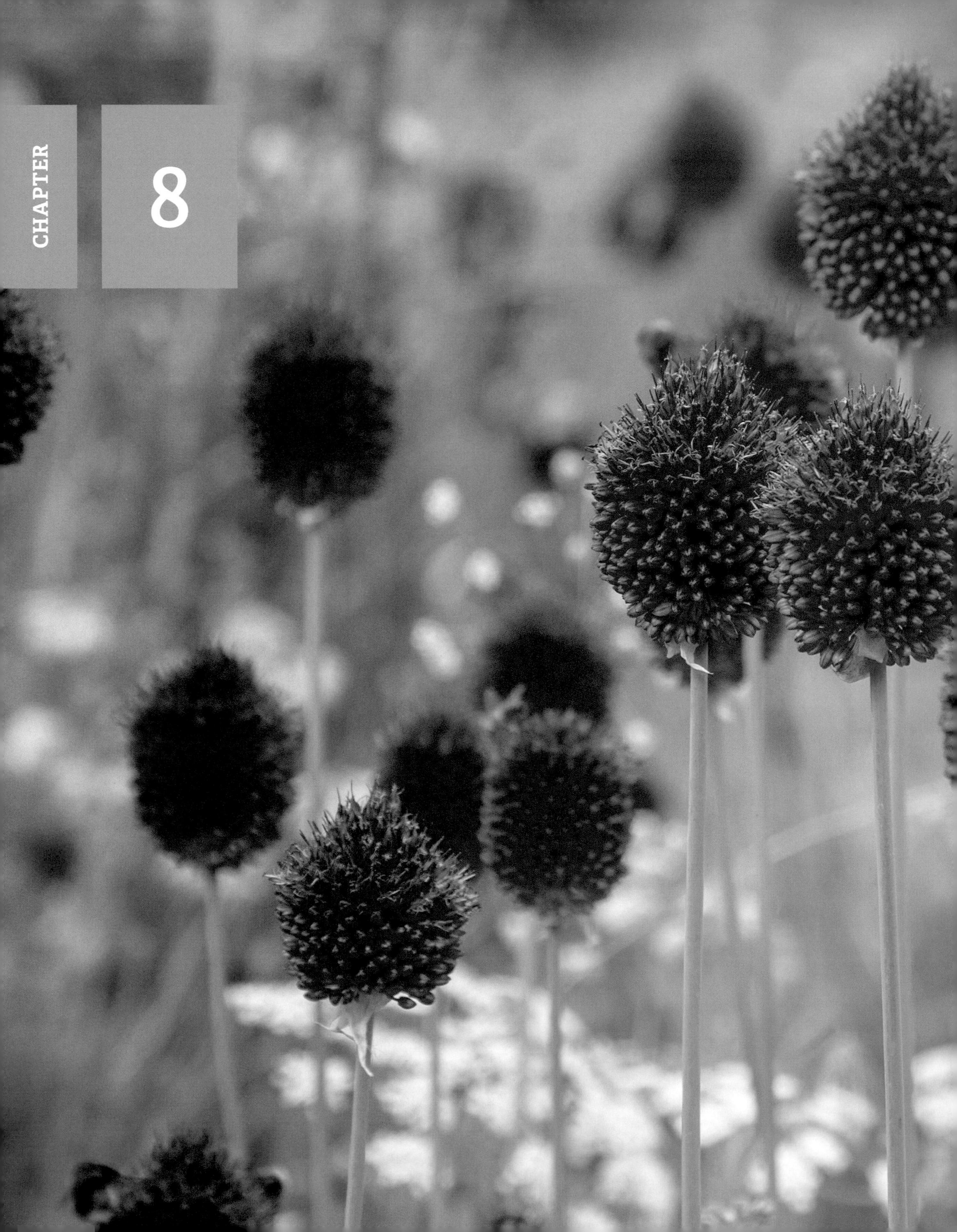

BULBS

No flowers bring me more pleasure than those that push up into the sunlight from spring-flowering bulbs. Perhaps it's *when* the bulbs bloom that makes them so special. To be cheered after cold, dark winter days by a daffodil in late winter never fails to pierce me with pleasure—and this is coming from a gardener who has ample blooms and color during the winter months. It is the promise of spring that makes even nongardeners want to garden, and bulbs embody that promise.

At one time, I thought of bulbs only as spring blooms—those bulbs I devoutly planted in the ground each fall and awaited in spring. It's not that I didn't know of other winter-, summer-, and fall-blooming bulbs. I just never really thought of those flowers as bulbs. It's silly, I know.

For winter flowers, I've planted *Galanthus*, those happy January blooming varieties also known as snowdrops. The common name is correct, in that they do indeed look like snow ready to drop. Over the years, gladiolus, calla lilies, tuberous begonias, and dahlias are bulbs that have all found homes in my summer gardens. Come autumn, my fall garden is filled with saffron crocuses and red spider lilies (*Lycoris radiata*), and I have even had some luck with *Colchicums* (often referred to as autumn crocus, although it is not a crocus). But still when I think of bulbs, I think of the fall as the time to prepare for much-anticipated spring.

Alliums add beautiful pops of color to a spring garden.

Bulbs can bring splashes of color and joy to every season, including summer.

Not all bulbs are the same. There are five types of bulbs falling under that title: true bulbs, corms, tubers, rhizomes, and tuberous roots. It's a good idea to understand the differences, but it's also OK to call them all bulbs. Or at least I think it is.

- **True bulbs** contain a fully formed plant. Daffodils, tulips, lilies, grape hyacinths, and amaryllis are all true bulbs. If you slice open a daffodil vertically, you will find the entire embryonic daffodil—flower, stem, leaves, and roots—ready to spring forth once the time is right. True bulbs can be annuals or perennials.

- **Corms** are similar to true bulbs, in that they contain a stem base, but they do not hold the entire baby plant. The roots growing from a basal plate are located on the bottom of the corm. (The basal plate is the base area of the bulb.) The growth point is located on the top of the corm. A corm only lasts for a single season, but a new corm will form on top of the old one. Cormels (which can be separated from the parent to grow new plants) are also produced, forming around the base of the corm's basal plate. Popular corms include gladiolus and crocuses.
- **Tubers** have an underground stem base, with no basal plate. Roots of the tuber grow from both the base and from the sides, with multiple growth points spread out over the tuber's surface. Classic examples are anemones and caladiums.
- **Rhizomes** are thickened stems that grow either partly or completely underground. If you immediately thought of a bearded iris, you are correct. On a rhizome, the largest growth point is located at one end, with additional growth points located along the sides. Most of us are able to clearly identify these bulbs as rhizomes.
- **Tuberous roots** are the fifth and final type of bulb. Most often, tuberous roots are not thought of as bulbs at all (at least, not by me), but they are. Their parts below the ground are unmistakable. Unlike other bulb types, tuberous roots have puffy root-like structures that look as though someone pumped them up like a balloon. These are actually adapted stems—not true roots. Instead, the actual root grows from the sides and the tip of the tuberous root. Familiar tuberous root plants include dahlias and daylilies.

When styling your garden at home, there is no reason not to have bulbs blooming during every month of the year. The variety available is astounding. I had so many summer-blooming bulbs, but I never actually thought of them as bulbs. In the end, I don't suppose it mattered, as long as I enjoyed watching the hummingbirds sipping nectar from cthe annas, wondered at the twisting red and yellow petals of the glory lily (*Gloriosa superba*), or admired the crocosmia floating across the gravel path.

Now, I will wait to see these wonders rise each month and accept them all as bulbs.

The Basics of Forcing Spring Flower Bulbs

Aside from not liking the term "forcing," I enjoy getting bulbs to bloom indoors to jump-start spring. I don't do this on a massive level, but I like to have a few around, brightening a January day. Even if they are already blooming outside, I like having the flowers inside as well.

Since a true bulb contains everything it needs to bloom the first year, no additional nutrients are needed. This is why you see hyacinths blooming in those cute, specially designed glass containers. However, without added nutrients, the bulb will not return again. So, after it blooms, you should place it in the compost pile.

Bulbs will need excellent drainage. Choose a container with a drainage hole and fill it with planting medium (within 2 inches [5.1cm] of the rim for larger bulbs and closer to the rim for smaller bulbs).

Arrange the bulbs on the planting medium with the pointed end up. It's better to crowd them so they are almost touching. We want to make a statement, so let's make it! Once positioned, the tops of the bulbs should all be level, about ½ inch (1.3cm) from the surface. Backfill with more planting medium so the bulb tips are just barely poking out.

Place the pots in a chilling area, ideally in a low-light or darkened space. This period will be dependent on the bulb—you will need anywhere from 12 to 16 weeks of chilling. Keep the bulbs evenly moist but not in standing water. Good drainage is important.

Once they sprout, gradually give the bulbs warmer temperatures and light. Place them where you can enjoy them the most.

CONTAINER GARDENS

Container gardens can be lush with vibrant berries, a single species, or a mix of plants that create a miniature landscape, allowing you to flex your horticultural muscle in a small space—the container—with minimal effort.

You can place container gardens to create beauty and diversity in a range of spaces: on a balcony, porch, deck, pool, window box, or even in perennial borders. A raised container can add rhythm and height to your garden beds. You also add versatility when you consider how you'll be viewing the container garden—you can arrange containers to make any point of view more interesting. Portability is another benefit to the use of containers; you can move them around to take advantage of either shade or sunlight.

For a simple clapboard house, two large urns flanking the front entrance and filled with cottage garden plants can be enough to evoke all the charm of a full-fledged cottage garden. For a modern home, try offering architectural interest; a sculptural, shaped glazed pot planted with a stunning plant may be all the space needs. Adding any more to a modern space may spoil the impact. If you have a traditional-style home, you can't go wrong with a pair of containers setting a symmetrical stage to greet your visitors—or even a large single pot for an asymmetric punctuation point. Containers grouped on the deck or patio can be very effective, creating an individual design statement. Grouping containers also makes it easy to

Unique pots add an aesthetic element to your garden design.

trade out plants that aren't looking their best. Every home and garden style can benefit from a container garden to complement its individual look.

When choosing plants for your container garden, include plants with similar cultural conditions, such as light and watering needs. Also, consider each plant's growth rate. Ideally, the growth rate during the season should be similar so one plant will not dominate the container later in the year.

When choosing a container, select the largest pot within your budget that also fits the space and your overall aesthetic. Containers need to be watered frequently, so the larger the pot, the less frequently you will need to water. During the heat of the summer, containers may need watering once a day. If the containers are small, having to water twice a day is not uncommon.

Because of the contained space, nutrients will leach out with each watering. It's important to fill container gardens with a quality potting mix and blend in a slow-release fertilizer to replenish the nutrients during the season. Top-dress your pot with mulch to decorate, reduce splashing, and retain moisture.

Mulch can be much more than purely functional. Mulch can be an extension of your personality, so be creative.

Simple wood and bark mulches work fine, but consider shells, pebbles, marbles, or any material you might have available, even acorns. It all depends on the look you are trying to achieve. Once the planting is complete, consider adding an accent to finish the design. For example, add a bunny, bird, seashell, or frog, as long as it is in keeping with the scale of the design.

Even if you don't have much space to work with, you can get your gardening fix by planting your garden in a container. When it comes to flexibility, ability to experiment and have fun, and injecting beauty and color into your views, container gardening is the way to go.

When creating container gardens, consider them as making a cameo appearance during a thrilling opera. It's your chance to be witty, charming, or themed with herbs, scents, or vegetables. Herbs and vegetables can be placed on a sunny back porch just a snip away from the cook's hand. Scented gardens can be created in an enclosed area, accentuating the aromas from the potted garden. Container gardens can offer a welcome surprise as you round a corner or can be used for privacy to block an awkward view of a neighbor. And as an added bonus, if your experiment should fail, it's easy enough to pull the plants and start again.

GARDENING WITH CONFIDENCE

Try Hypertufa

Some of my favorite container gardens are made from hypertufa troughs—homemade faux stone containers modeled after ancient stone troughs once used in England to hold water and feed for livestock. During a recent visit to Wave Hill, Bronx, New York, I was enchanted by alpines I saw planted in hypertufas, grouped as if they were on a craggy ledge. Individually they were interesting; clustered together they were a work of art.

I learned to make hypertufa troughs from friends Beth Jimenez and Amelia Lane, owners of Lasting Impressions in Raleigh, North Carolina, when working on a how-to story for *Country Gardens* magazine. A grouping of these containers in various sizes makes a striking garden collection.

Container gardening works especially well for growing herbs and lettuces close to your kitchen.

COTTAGE AND COUNTRY GARDENS

Roses on arbors, vines on trellises, and pink peonies and blue larkspur against white picket fences—the images that come to mind of bygone days and summer breezes, of quaint gardens with old-fashioned plants and a comfortable ambiance. These are the things that, for most of us, typify a cottage or country garden. But don't be limited to those usual elements. If you can imagine it, it can become part of your cottage or country garden.

The origins of the cottage garden and country garden were different. Cottage gardens had humble beginnings—ordinary English people began creating practical gardens surrounding their working-class cottages. Country gardens were pockets of small cottage-style gardens on the large estates of the upper-class gentry.

The terms "cottage" and "country" at one time described two very different kinds of garden. Cottage gardens were quaint and charming way to make a cottage home complete. With limited space, cottage gardens needed a firm hand to make the best use of their space. Country gardens, however, were in many ways an attempt to provide a place for quiet repose closer to the home, providing smaller spaces within the vastness of an estate. Today, the terms are often used interchangeably, though there still exist some distinctions between them.

To get a clearer understanding of what cottage and country gardens represent

This wooden bench is the type of rustic element that works well in a cottage or country garden.

45

today, I turned to my friend, then-editor of *Country Gardens* magazine, James Augustus Baggett. His comment does a nice job of capturing the essence, "To me, Cottage is a style of gardening, and Country is a spirit. . . . . When I think of a Cottage garden, I think of gardens with strong bones, an imposed design, perhaps even a bit on the formal side, filled with exuberant bloomers. . . . Country gardens are equally blowsy and filled with old-fashioned favorites, but with a personal twist: the incorporation of found objects or architectural salvage, repurposed materials, even sculpture and artwork. . . . I like to say that you can have a Country garden on 40 acres or 40 stories high."

Cottage Gardens

The cottage garden is a distinct style and one that, to me, refers to the cottage-style house poking through the garden. Cottage gardens evoke romance and nostalgia. A cottage garden can have formal elements or a relaxed, informal style. In both cases, the gardens are filled with herbs and soft fruiting trees or with roses that cause you to duck as you enter through the arbor gate.

Rich in history, the cottage garden evokes grace and charm. In the beginning, this gardening style stemmed from practicality. Fences, iconic in cottage garden design, were used to keep livestock out, not as a backdrop for pretty flowers or to frame the garden, as fences are most often used today. Garden space was used to grow plants the family needed for both medicine and cooking flavors. Flowers, especially reseeding ones or pass-along plants, were used to fill spaces between herbs and veggies. Roses have long been favored in cottage gardens. They are both pretty and edible, as long as they are without pesticides, which a cottage gardener would not dare to use.

Cottage gardens had a purpose, related to good health and pollination. Although cottage gardens are still filled with purpose, more often than not, today they are grown to soothe the soul rather than to serve apothecary needs. The beauty of a cottage gardens is reason enough to have one.

Country Gardens

The English have long presented country gardens with a formal flair through their use of lengthy, straight bed edges with a swath of turf separating them. Inside the formal edges are informal plantings in a controlled chaos, creating sensory delights.

That is how I would describe my garden. My years living in England were the most influential in molding my gardening style. The plantings inside the formal beds of my country garden are exuberant as they spill over their formal frame to lighten the mood and relax the style.

Country gardens lend themselves to accents such as a sundial, or rustic elements like an old tractor seat transformed into a solitary garden chair. Butterflies formed out of old sheet metal, architectural bits added for age and wear, and other whimsical and personal touches add the kind of character often admired in country gardens. I like country gardens for that very reason.

Regional influences and personal style give country gardens even more charm. For example, a seashell-studded birdbath, though a welcome addition to any garden, would make a fitting accent to a country garden in Maine, where seashells may be readily obtainable. Most accents in a country garden will be found objects or items constructed out of locally available materials.

Today, the lines between cottage and country gardens have blurred. In fact, they may be better described as cottage country gardens. Both are charming and evoke a personal connection between garden and gardener. Either style, or an interweaving of the two, is certain to make your garden into a quaint, enjoyable space.

No matter which garden style you prefer, open lawn space is nice to have.

GARDENING WITH CONFIDENCE

Create the Space You Want

To my dismay, my house style is not strictly a cottage or country style. I have worked hard to tone down the formal style of my home with less formal colors and accents. So, by definition, my house and garden are probably now more along the lines of a country style—except for the weird trees and few pieces of contemporary garden art I collect.

We don't always have the home and garden we dream of making. In my mind, my dream home and garden are perched along the English Channel, at Dover perhaps, dangerously near the White Cliffs. The house is white with a pale blue roof and a white picket fence. There's an arbor above the entrance gate with an 'Old Blush' rose dangling down, leaving pink petals on my sleeve whenever I pass under it. The wind blows, throwing my hair back as if I were in a photo shoot. (And, since I'm in my imagination, my hair is still the chestnut brown of my youth.)

We can and should create what we want, even if we have to stretch reality just a bit. So even though no one who has ever visited my garden thinks of it as country, to me it is. It always will be. Free and happy, settled and chaotic—a place I call home. Or, to reiterate what James has said, "Country is a spirit . . . you can have a Country garden on 40 acres or 40 stories high."

FORMAL AND INFORMAL GARDENS

We each have internal wiring, I believe, that sets our comfort zone in one of two camps: formal or informal. As much as I like all styles, I will gravitate toward formal first. Always. I've tried changing my stripes, but I've never had any success. It is good to know your preference so that, when you are designing your garden, you can plan with your own tastes in mind. Don't let anyone talk you into something different because it won't work for you.

No doubt you will intuitively do what comes naturally to you, pairing up pots or setting one askew. You already have an inkling about which camp you fall into. Any garden design can emphasize the formal or informal. Even if your home layout is formal, it doesn't mean you have to stick to that. Put your personal, informal touch into the gardens. Knowing about these two categories of style and your own preferences will make you more confident in your choices.

Formal

Clean lines, clarity of composition, and notable structure help characterize formal designs. What defines a formal garden is incorporating bold geometric shapes and classic symmetry. Formal designs can be found anywhere and used in any garden setting, from rural gardens to suburban lots. Even a balcony garden can be formal in style.

This formal garden has a defined patio and lawn.

Formal contemporary gardens often use geometric shapes to echo the home's design. Whether these shapes are rectangular, circular, or square, repeating them elsewhere in the landscape design—such as in pools, patios, beds, and borders—will add to the formality of the design.

Symmetry plays an important role in formal design. A classic use of symmetry is mirroring on one side of the garden what appears on the other side. Relying on symmetry and geometric shapes in the overall design and then keeping the design simple, clean, and spare will define your formal garden. Choose plantings that will enhance the symmetry and geometry.

A matching pair of planted containers at the home's entrance says formal, no matter what's planted within. It is the shapes, lines, and symmetry that provide the formality and not the plantings. Taking what we think of as naturalistic plants and using them *en masse* works well in a formal design, as long as the formality of the design is present.

Using masses of single species, recurring colors, forms, and foliage will add rhythm to a garden design, clarifying the unity and cohesion—all helping to define a formal landscape. Just remember to keep the design in balance for a more consistent look.

While other garden design styles come and go, formal landscape designs have never gone out of favor. This is due, in part, to the ability to add formality to any type of planting design. Even naturalistic gardens can be formal by design. Generally, formal spaces are less concerned with displaying plant collections than staying true to the governing rules of this design style.

Using a palette of native plants in a formal way makes it possible to paint a new picture of the American landscape. Today, more and more people are turning to native plants for their adaptability in the landscape and benefits to the wildlife.

Most people don't consider natives for use in a formal design. We tend to choose plants based on preconceived notions that certain plants should only be used in certain types of themed gardens. Moss, for example, is too often considered a weed in the lawn, when this native should be embraced as a lawn replacement to add a relaxed yet formal feeling to a shady, native garden design. Other great natives that can be used in a formal way are *Panicum virgatum* 'Shenandoah', an ornamental grass you can group in a formal bed, or Oakleaf hydrangea, *Hydrangea quercifolia*, which can be sheared in a formal way.

Stay True to Your Gardening Personality

My home is built with a very formal design with a center door and an equal number of windows on either side. Since I like formal design, it made it easy for me to use the house's form and symmetry as a starting point. However, I don't like fussy formal. My style leans toward the casual. To keep the house and garden cohesive, instead of mirroring one side on the other, I mimicked them. As I placed a tree on the left, I also placed another tree on the right. Instead of being the same, they were of equal height and relative weight. The lines of the beds are rectangular, as are the lines of the house, but the plantings in the beds are curved, loose, and perhaps even a bit chaotic. It's a look that works for me; it allows me to work off the style of the house while at the same time bringing in my own gardening personality.

Whether you lean toward a formal or an informal garden design, stay true to yourself. Designing the garden strictly based on the style of the house may not give you the garden you want. In the end, the design will please you more if it actually reflects your personality and your preferences.

This garden design is a bit more informal and relaxed.

Break the old rules suggesting that only certain plants work in formal design. Experiment with plants, and don't be afraid to try your own ideas about the plants you'd like to use. The lines of the design are what keep a formal garden formal.

Informal

Informal design can be thought of as the opposite of formal style. An informal garden will have a more relaxed design achieved through curved lines and irregular shapes. The plantings tend to be looser with a more naturalistic and asymmetrical pattern and placement of design elements. Rustic-looking elements, such as galvanized tubs planted with herbs, grapevine wreaths, and planters made from an old pair of gardening shoes, will feel natural here since the space is less rigid.

Many home styles have informal lines—they're asymmetrical, with the side to the left of the front door being different from the side to the right of the front door. These lines suggest the garden design to follow suit. Instead of a pair of matching containers gracing the front door as would be appropriate in a formal design, you can use containers in an unmatched way. This could be as simple as having just one large pot in scale with the home on the side that needs balancing. For example, if the home is one story on one side of the door and rises to a second level on the other, adding an urn on the single-story side helps balance the asymmetrical lines. Or the weight of a pairing could mimic the lines of the home with one side supporting one large urn and the other side displaying a grouping of containers.

For informal design, matching one side to the other may not be the norm, it is still OK to do. More often, the lines of an asymmetrical home allows the plantings to balance the lines. Following the example of the home with one side taller than the other, a tree planted in front of the single-story side will balance the two sides, bringing height to the side with the second story.

In many ways, designing an informal garden takes more thought than designing a formal garden (which may seem counterintuitive). It's much easier to mirror an image to complement a formal design than it is to balance the lines of an asymmetrical layout. If you think in terms of balancing the weight from one side to the other, the design will be more cohesive.

GARDENS OUT FRONT

Sweeping beds lining the driveway with flowers nodding to you as you return home . . . vegetables nestled next to your ornamental plants, flanking both sides of the entrance path . . . a fence backdrop to a wildlife buffet—wherever your desires take you, front yard gardens are gaining long-overdue attention.

Somewhere along the way, we absorbed the idea that gardens in the front were designed to be constant. Little risk was taken with perennials or deciduous trees and shrubs. Today, gardens in the front of the house are being viewed with new eyes. Gardeners can explore new potential with diverse plantings for seasonal change and for the wildlife. It is no longer forbidden to think of adding vegetables in beds or mixing them in with perennials. With times changing, as styles are more relaxed and practical, why not garden out front?

Others prefer a private retreat, creating an oasis only for those who enter the garden to enjoy that can't be seen from the street. It takes just a little confidence to understand the potential and overcome old beliefs that gardens out front should be static.

Look beyond the front garden as a place with only evergreens, appearing the same in February as in August. Add diversity with deciduous trees and shrubs, flowering vines, annuals, perennials, and vegetables to allow the full range of interest to peak as the seasons turn. You will appreciate each season every time you come and go.

This lush garden by the driveway helps balance the space in front of the home.

Take your cue from your home's style—is it a cottage, ranch, contemporary, or formal home? Matching the style of the front garden to the front of your house is simply a matter of observing carefully and thinking about what you have and what you'd like to have. Evaluate your home's style with a critical eye. Note the material (brick, clapboard, stone), color (door, trim, windows, embellishments), and any distinctive style elements (roof lines, linear lines, porch railings, etc.). For example, cottage style homes give rise to welcoming, informal garden designs. Daylilies lining the driveway can welcome you during the height of the summer season. A long, low ranch will beg for knee-hugging plants, such as herbaceous peonies, which bloom for only a couple of weeks a year but are incomparable. A rustic-style home will relax with a similarly styled garden featuring old-fashioned native plants like black-eyed Susans. A red door will need red flowers to echo its hello. Likewise, introduce other colors into your garden to complement your home's colors.

Vegetables Out Front?

Not everyone has the freedom to do anything they want in the yard out front. Many homeowner associations prohibit certain plantings, such as vegetable gardens. Fortunately for me, there is no restriction in my community barring front yard vegetable gardens. There is a marked trend among gardeners toward putting formerly static land to work.

When we were looking for a place to put in a vegetable garden, the best sun was located at the top of our driveway in the front yard. It's not very big area, measuring only 20 feet (6.1m) square and with a black wrought-iron fence segregating it from the rest of the front yard. Even though it's out front, however, it's coincidentally in a discreet location, hidden behind the cars.

Having the vegetable garden out front allows us to see the garden every time we go to and from the cars. We can clearly see when weeding is needed, when our vegetables ripen, and if watering or other maintenance is needed. When we want a tomato for dinner, it's easy to pick one as we walk inside to start supper. Would you put a vegetable garden in your own front yard?

A front garden can be a place to engage, always open for conversation with your neighbors.

Embellish the front garden with seating, fencing, arbors, or even a gazebo. The front space can be public or private or a combination of both. Add fencing to provide a backdrop for your garden and, at the same time, offer a sense of security. Show your style to others and express yourself by creating a lovely and welcoming garden out front.

HERBS

HERB GARDENS

While visiting a friend's garden, you may brush against a rosemary bush, and a comforting memory of your mother's garden might come to mind. Suddenly, you remember her roasted chicken seasoned with rosemary. When you plant an herb garden, you cultivate more than plants; you cultivate a legacy of memories.

Herbs can be intermingled with your flowers and vegetables or planted in a dedicated herb garden. They grow well in the ground, in containers, and even in window boxes. Growing herbs knows no trend. In both ancient and modern times, herbs have been used for seasoning and scent, as well as for creating medicinal and housekeeping concoctions.

Herbs require little care, if given the right conditions. To begin your herb garden, find a location in your yard that receives full sun. Most herbs need six to eight hours of sun a day. Another requirement is well-drained soil; they don't like to have their feet wet. One a side note, locating your herb garden within easy access will encourage you to use it.

Some herbs are annuals—that is, plants that complete their life cycles in one year. Basils and dill are annuals. Some herbs, such as parsley, are biennial—that is, plants that complete their life cycles in two years, typically setting seed the second year. Parsley will self-sow, as well, keeping your pantry well supplied. Many other herbs are perennials— that is, plants that last at least three life cycles, such as rosemary, lavender, chives, oregano,

There is a lot of value to be had from a wooden raised-bed herb garden.

57

sage, tarragon, and thyme. When you have an herb garden with annuals, biennials, and perennials, it makes it easy to create a garden with year-round interest. Not only do they add scent and seasoning, but herbs also possess attractive leaves and texture, provide pollen for bees, and can play host to butterflies.

When the late afternoon draws near and dinner is being prepared, gather a sprig of rosemary from close at hand. Whether fresh from your garden or previously picked and now dried and sitting ready to use in a jar on your kitchen shelf, your own herbs will enhance your meal and build memories for generations to come.

Harvesting Herbs

- Cut sprigs or branches in the morning after the dew has evaporated and before the heat of the day. Herb oils are at their highest concentration during the morning hours, and these oils produce aroma and flavor.
- Harvest herbs for drying just as the first flower buds begin to open, when the oils in the leaves are most concentrated. This will yield peak flavor that will last once preserved.
- Use a sharp knife, pruning scissors, or clippers to cut branches for drying.
- Right after harvesting, wash gently in cool water and dry in the open air.

GARDENING WITH CONFIDENCE

Herb Gardens with Style

Herb gardens can be formal with traditional accents like a sundial or armillary. You can arrange them in a tight, geometric knot garden, or they can be footloose and fancy-free in a casual plot where anything goes.

One of my favorite herb gardens is The Little Herb House, in Raleigh, North Carolina. The entire area measures 100 feet (30.5m) square, and gravel paths radiate from a centered, two-tiered millstone fountain, splashing sound around eight display gardens with names like Flower Arranger, Old Geezer, Sage and Salvia, Healing Tea, and Potpourri. Each of the different herbal themes includes fun and whimsical garden accents. In the Butterfly and Bee Garden are large swaths of echinacea (cone flowers) and monarda (bee balm) dancing around the cutest bird feeder and a welcoming bath. Garden accents are the perfect pairing with herbs.

Herbs can be planted in galvanized containers if you're low on space or simply like the style.

Harvesting Seeds
- Herbs grown for the seeds should be harvested when the seed heads turn brown.
- Bundle and tie the seed heads and put them in lunch-sized paper bags for drying. Add a few holes in the sides of the bags for air circulation.
- The seeds are ready when they loosen and fall out when you shake the seed heads. Store in airtight jars.

Drying Herbs
- To dry herbs in small bundles, tie them together at the ends, and hang them upside down in a warm, dry, well-ventilated location, out of direct sunlight.
- Keep the bundles small and somewhat loose so the air can circulate. The attic, shed, or garage are all good locations for drying.
- To dry herbs on a rack, lay the branches in a single layer on a drying rack.
- Once the leaves feel crisp, usually in a week or less, strip the leaves from the stems and store in airtight jars.
- Before storing, always make sure your herbs are completely dry. It will take a few days. When in doubt, leave them out to dry another day or two more.

MOSS GARDENING

Emerald-green rolling mounds, stillness-enticing and barefoot-begging, mosses evoke a special feeling like no other plant on earth. Used as a lawn replacement for shady locations, ground cover in woodland gardens, or even in decorative dish gardens, mosses are gracing more home gardens today than ever before.

Primitive plants that evolved 450 million years ago (70 million years before ferns and tens of millions more years before the first dinosaur), mosses are finally getting their due.

As homeowners look toward less maintenance and more environmentally friendly practices, they're realizing that in a shady spot, mosses are the epitome of "green." With few demands, moss, once established, rarely needs watering, and requires no fertilization. Plus, it will eventually knit together, suppressing weeds.

Most mosses prefer a moist, shady spot. The commonly held belief is that they require an acid pH range of 5.0 to 5.5, but actually, mosses will thrive in a wide pH range, not just acidic. It is more correct to say that other plants don't prefer pH levels of 5.0 to 5.5, so there is less competition, allowing moss colonization.

Although most mosses prefer shady woodland settings, there are others that like a range of climates, from the *Bryum argenteum* growing in the cracks of sidewalks to the *Tortula muralis* found in desert regions or

Two little faces pop up in a lush moss garden.

Ferns and other forest greenery work well in moss gardens.

the *Campylopus introflexus* growing in coastal regions. Rhizoids, not roots, are what attaches moss to the ground. Because mosses have no roots, amending the substrate isn't necessary: moss will grow on compacted soil or even clay.

As a nonvascular plant, mosses are so primitive they get what they need from the environment. They receive their moisture from the boundary layer of the soil, rain, dew, and even fog; nutrients and water move from cell to cell by osmosis. During times of drought, mosses go dormant.

Mosses come in both clumping (acrocarpus spp.) and spreading (pleurocarpous spp.) forms.

The clumping forms, or the acrocarps, are generally recommended for borders. They act as living mulch between plants or under trees, in areas where their quilting, mounding, three-dimensional effect can be appreciated.

For lawns, **the spreading forms**, or the pleurocarps, are commonly recommended for their ability to a form a seamless carpet. *Hypnum imponens* (sheet moss), *Plagiomnium cuspidatum* (woodsy mnium), and *Thuidium delicatulum* (fern moss) are good choices for shady lawn replacement. These have low profiles, produce spreading, fast-growing colonies, and a prostrate habit. It's best to add more than one species to increase the chances of a moss liking its location and forming a dominate colony.

In spite of a preference for moist sites, you can encourage mosses to colonize in places that aren't naturally moist by

GARDENING WITH CONFIDENCE

Moss Is a Blessing

Moss has always intrigued me. It seemed to just show up. It fills the cracks between my stone pavers on the north side of my home, adding age and interest.

About half the time I meet people and the conversation turns to moss, they ask my opinion on how to remove it. Most often the questions are about moss lawns. They are bothered because moss is invading their lawns—their words, not mine. When I hear this, an eyebrow usually rises as I pause for the right diplomatic words to gracefully ask, "Why would you want to do that?"

Consider yourself lucky if moss is in your lawn. If it happens, work at removing the struggling grass, and you will have a no-mow, no-pest, emerald-green ground cover. You will not need to remember when to fertilize or have any of the common anxieties associated with building the perfect lawn.

lightly irrigating the area to allow for colonization. Once established, mosses don't need irrigation. Keeping them irrigated will hasten the growth process and add intrigue as you watch various mosses vie for the fiefdom. For even more interest, add woodland wildflowers to your moss, such as creeping phlox (*Phlox subulata*), foam flowers (*Tiarella* spp.), or Oconee bells (*Shortia galacifolia*).

Mosses' tiny leaves are vulnerable in that they don't have the waxy cuticles of vascular plants, absorbing rain or dew directly through the leaf surface. Mosses convert sunlight into energy using chlorophyll, but because moss is on such a small scale, even a small fallen tree leaf can inhibit their growth. As such, keep mossy areas free of long-standing debris.

Mosses reproduce through spores and leaf fragmentation. Spore season is one of the most magical times in a moss garden. Leaning low to see a stand of moss spores is a rewarding moment, engaging even the most hardened soul.

In planning a design, know that moss gardens tolerate occasional foot traffic; mosses are not as delicate as they look. However, in areas of frequent traffic, be sure to include stepping stones.

Adding moss, which is green as it was "in the beginning," will bring a new perspective to your garden, making what is old new again.

ROCK GARDENING

My gardening philosophy has always been, "More is better; lush is life." I never imagined I would ever become a rock gardener. But then I attended meetings of the local chapter of the North American Rock Garden Society (NARGS) because it's widely known that the group has the very best programs, and they lured me in.

If you want to learn about plants and have time to join only one garden club, then join NARGS. Rock gardeners are a serious group of gardeners. Not evangelical, like many other types of gardeners, but intense and committed to the tiniest of plants grouped in a bunch of rocks with the hopes that their stratifications look natural.

When I announced on my Facebook page that I had become a rock gardener, my friend and fellow rock gardener Bobby Ward, NARGS's executive secretary, wrote in the comment section, "Glad you finally heard the calling!" Yes, I heard *my* calling. This may sound a bit smug on Bobby's part, but it wasn't meant to be. It's a known fact that rock gardeners are snobs. They have a reason to be since they are among the best gardeners around. Bobby is in good company, too. Southern garden writer Elizabeth Lawrence says in her book *A Rock Garden in the South*, "Some snobbery is to be expected, for all are agreed that the cultivation of rock plants is the highest form of the art of gardening."

So, in 2010, I went over to the other side of the lush life and joined this elite society. I still

Rock gardens make a lovely showcase for greenery.

can't believe they let me in. Like any garden group, the interest ranges from casual to committed. The definition of a rock garden, from the casual rock gardener's perspective (that is, my own perspective), is as simple as plants growing in rocky soil. To the committed rock gardeners who write their own definitions, there are no rules.

For me, the most important requirements are to grow plants in my rock garden that are small in size and are in scale with the surrounding rocks or stones. I prefer plants to be less than 15 inches (38.1cm) tall.

This is the place for the tiniest aquilegias and other perennials, the smallest bulbs, very slow-growing conifers,

and plants that might be smothered in areas where larger plants grow. The rock garden is an area viewed best on a raised level, perhaps using a berm or trough to raise the height of the plants. This garden can be in sun or shade. Build it with or without large rocks. Success depends on perspective and proportion.

The location I chose for my rock garden had been the herb garden. It was sloped, facing west, with poor soil. I was ready for a new challenge. I was fortunate to have natural slope in my garden, but in its absence, creating a berm would have worked as well. I added cobble-sized rocks, soil, and pine conditioner. Then

GARDENING WITH CONFIDENCE

Follow Your Heart

Adding the rock garden to my home garden, was the first thing I ever did that drew my husband's attention to my gardening. His comments weren't flattering—something to do with moonscapes. Admittedly, a ton of pea gravel can look like that. From my perspective, he just lacked vision. If he'd sat in on a NARGS lecture or toured a member's garden, I was sure he would've quickly grasped the appeal and suggested other areas we could convert.

Eighteen months later, the pea gravel in my rock garden is barely an accent under the alpine plants. It's gorgeous, and I've not heard a peep from my husband, which tells me it must be acceptable.

Follow your heart and pursue your vision. Criticism may come—ignore it unless it's from a fellow NARGS "enlightened one." If you like it, build it, and make us all proud. For more information on NARGS, go to *https://www.nargs.org/*.

This rock garden is filled with spring-flowering plants.

I top-dressed the whole garden with gravel. I also brought in larger stones to use for visual interest and to pair with my plantings. And I was very careful to ensure the stratifications in my rocks were straight and looked natural.

After I made my announcement of becoming a rock gardener, other friends wrote to say they were not surprised since, as Elizabeth Lawrence writes, "All gardeners become rock gardeners if they garden long enough." This is not to say I will no longer garden for wildlife. I will. And I do still love large, lusty blooms—the bigger the better. But now I've carved out one section of my garden to make a rock garden. Now, I see petite plants that stand on their own to fascinate me and allow for new discovery.

Some of my favorite rock gardens share similarities, including the addition of dwarf conifers to add vertical interest, giving the illusion that the landscape isn't a miniature. However, they all intrigue me, whether in crevices, on berms, or even planted in hypertufa troughs; adding low-growing plants that can be viewed individually is impressive to me. Rock gardens may be an acquired taste, but for me, so was coffee. Today, it's the first thing on my mind when I wake in the morning.

CHAPTER

16

VEGETABLE GARDENS

Have you ever tasted a tomato picked fresh from the vine, still warm from the summer sun? If you have, I'm sure you look forward to more. If you're not sure, then most likely you haven't—you would clearly remember.

Having food fresh from our own gardens is a growing trend. By producing our own food, we are also helping the environment by reducing "food miles"; we need only step into the garden to get seasonal veggies. This season you can prepare your garden space and start to enjoy fresh vegetables from just a little patch of land. Best of all, you get to choose what you want to grow and eat!

Lucky is the gardener who has some space to grow veggies. They can be planted in separate beds, raised or in the ground, or comingled with existing ornamental plants. You can plant your vegetables in neat rows or circles or zigzags. As long as you don't have to maximize your harvest, you can let your imagination run wild.

Vegetable gardens do have a couple of requirements. You will need a sunny spot with at least six hours of sun for your plants to grow strong and healthy. Many veggies can even be grown in containers, making them easy to move around if needed to keep them in sunlight (or if you have limited space, such as in a balcony garden). It's a good idea to locate the garden near the end of the hose or near a harvestable rain source. Watering is a must for a vegetable garden, so plan ahead and have

Rows of herbs, flowers, and vegetables create a garden with an air of abundance.

water easily accessible; you will need it on days when it doesn't rain.

I've set up my vegetable garden in a spot where I can direct the rain from the roof to my bed. The garden, however, needs a consistent supply of water, and in the absence of rain, I provide supplemental moisture. Fortunately for us, our garden is in the front yard, keeping it visible so we can readily see if it needs watering.

Once you have identified the area for planting, prepare your ground by amending the existing soil—or soil you've brought in—with organic matter. No matter what type of soil you have, adding organic matter will improve the soil's texture by helping clay soils drain more easily and retaining moisture in sandy soils. Adding a layer of mulch over the entire area of your garden prevents weeds from sprouting, keeps soil moist, moderates the soil temperature, and gives a tidy look to the garden.

Some great vegetables for a beginner's garden are tomatoes, cucumbers, radishes, squash, peppers, and lettuce. Grow what you like to eat. No need to grow

tomatoes if you don't like them. When I make my plant selections each year, I choose varieties that are not readily available in the grocery store. Summer trips to the farmer's market provide me with common varieties. My precious space is used on varieties that are difficult to find.

Pest control plays an important part in any vegetable garden. The best pest control is picking the bugs right off the plant by hand and dropping them into a bucket of soapy water. Remember, you'll be eating this food. You wouldn't want to put into your mouth something coated with a chemical that just killed a bug, would you? Adding a birdbath and flowers near your vegetable garden will also encourage birds and beneficial insects to aid you in pest control.

Often, if you are having a problem with pests, others in your area are having similar problems. Your regional cooperative extension office is but a phone call or website visit away. Take advantage of this resource in your area.

Plan today for a bountiful vegetable harvest tomorrow. Once you taste the sun-warmed produce from the vine, you will be a vegetable grower for life.

Blend Practicality and Style

There's no reason your vegetable garden can't be productive and stylish. Too often vegetable gardens are relegated to the farthest part of the back garden—a place you can't monitor routinely that most likely requires you to drag a hose over for watering. Put your vegetable garden at the hub of your garden. Make it part of your daily, active life. You will find you use the garden more and can manage it better if it is located in a place where you can keep an eye on things. Staying on top of weed pulling, watering, and pest control goes a long way toward making it possible to enjoy the vegetable garden beyond the bounty of harvest time.

Vegetable gardens may need trellises or other elements that are functional but can also be opportunities to add style.

71

WILDLIFE GARDENS

As the evening light wanes, I step out the back door of my suburban home, entering my wildlife habitat. If I was seeking some alone time, I've come to the wrong place.

Many familiar friends are waiting for me. Butterflies fly above the heads of a resident box turtle, a few frogs, and a pair of anoles. Dragonflies avoid the praying mantis, the yellow garden spider weaves a web to welcome guests, and mosquitoes are being served for the bat buffet. Several birds are taking flight while others excitedly chirp away. I can hear bees buzzing, gathering their last bits of nectar and pollen before night falls. As I look around my wildlife habitat, I realize that each is here by invitation. It really is true—if you build it, they will come.

Creating a wildlife habitat is simple to do and richly rewarding. Your wildlife garden can be a container garden, a corner carved out of a traditional landscape, or an entire suburban lot. As we continue to look for ways to reduce lawn areas, making a sunny spot into a wildlife habitat is the perfect solution. Simply provide food, water, cover, and places for creatures to raise their young, and you will create a wildlife habitat.

To attract wildlife, supply the necessary kinds of food—either naturally or with supplements. The more food sources you have on hand, the greater the variety of creatures you'll attract. Various seeds, nuts, cones, berries, foliage, and fruits, as well as nectar, sap, and pollen, are all good food sources. Use

A North American black swallowtail butterfly enjoying the garden.

regional native plants, as they typically support 10 to 50 times more local wildlife than non-native plants. You can also supplement naturally occurring food with feeders that hold seeds, suet, or nectar.

Consider, too, the food needs of different types of wildlife at various stages of their life cycles. For example, the larvae of butterflies feed on specific host plants (depending on the type of butterfly), while the adults will sip the nectar of most flowers with an umbel shape (which creates an easy landing pad for feeding).

Water is essential for drinking and bathing, and a clean, reliable water source is key to creating a good habitat. Providing water can be as simple as adding a birdbath. Add multiple water spots, at varying heights, to attract a greater variety of wildlife. It is important to provide water year-round, even in the winter and especially during times of drought. Locate water sources where you can easily view them so they can entertain you, as well.

Wildlife needs cover for protection against the elements and predators. Having a place to escape the threat of impending danger will attract more little creatures to your garden. A variety of plant life—ranging in size, height, and density with trees, shrubs, perennials, annuals, vines, and ornamental grasses—will increase your chances of attracting more kinds of wildlife.

The cover will also give your wild friends a safe place for reproduction and for nurturing their young. In a backyard, dense shrubbery and nesting boxes provide safe havens for birds. Different animals have different needs; some animals require water to raise their young, such as salamanders, frogs, toads, and dragonflies.

Sustainable gardening practices will also benefit your wildlife habitat. Try to control non-native and invasive species, and eliminate or reduce the use of pesticides, herbicides, and fertilizers. It also helps to use mulch and reduce your lawn size, adding more sheltering and food plants for your wild visitors.

Take comfort in providing for the wildlife. With good, sustainable gardening practices, you are also creating a safe haven for yourself, as well. Invite wildlife to your garden; it's all the buzz!

A birdbath in the garden can become a hub of activity.

GARDENING WITH CONFIDENCE

Letting Go

In 1996, I became a mother. A lot changed for me that year, but nothing was more profound than the impact on me as a gardener. Not unlike statistics from the American Automobile Association reporting that women become better drivers after becoming mothers, I imagine that if a study were performed, it would find that new mothers also become safer gardeners, as do dads. It became increasingly important for me to build a garden where children could take part, not a place where I feared for them to tread.

In the past, I was hung up with perfection— no holes on the leaves, no bugs noshing my nasturtiums. As I proudly got rid of one pest, another always took its place.

Then I stopped. I stopped using anything, synthetic or organic, to rid the garden of pests.

The new garden, the one that I'm raising a family around today, is a place where everything is free—free of pesticides, fungicides, and herbicides; free of worry about holes in my leaves and bugs roaming uninhibited; free of fear that my kids might want to eat an unwashed fig from the tree. Within a year, the entire garden was in balance. Today, my garden is a menagerie of birds, bees, butterflies, snakes, frogs, and lizards. It's an ecosystem rather than a mere garden.

The decision to let nature take her course set me free.

You've probably seen the color wheel before in art class. The same principles can be used to great effect in the garden.

ADDING COLOR TO YOUR GARDEN

Color is what excites people most in a garden design—color in the flowers, the accents, and even in the furniture during the cold of winter. When visiting a garden with colors that blend, note what makes them work together. A refresher in color theory will make this easier to do.

Color Theory

Understanding color theory can help you make good decisions about your garden design. Use the color wheel for guidance to help you recognize why something looks great or just doesn't work:

- Primary colors are red, blue, and yellow. They share nothing in common. They are the colors from which all other colors are derived.
- Mixing two primary colors creates the secondary colors of green, purple, and orange.
- Combining a primary and a secondary color creates tertiary colors, such as yellow-green or orange-red.
- Analogous colors are those colors sitting next to each other on the color wheel. These colors blend easily with each other. For example, yellow with yellow-green and green is an analogous color combination.
- Contrasting colors (often called complementary colors) lie directly opposite each other on the color wheel. Examples include blue and orange, yellow and purple, and red and green. These color pairings intensify each other and make a bold statement when combined, offering a striking contrast.
- A harmonious color scheme uses contrasting colors with an added color that is analogous to one of the contrasting colors—for example using purple and yellow with yellow's neighbor, yellow-green.
- Monochromatic colors are those of a single tone, such as varying shades of blue. These have their place and can be the most calming of all garden styles.

Warm Colors

The warm colors, also known as hot colors, are energetic and vivid. Hot colors include red, orange, yellow, and the tertiary colors in between. These colors pair well with blue.

Warm colors reflect more light than they absorb, so they look bigger and closer than they actually are. Warm colors are considered active, attracting the eye. Visible from afar, warm colors dominate the scene and bring excitement and energy to the garden. Warm colors draw the eye to a focal point, such as a mailbox bed or an otherwise special area in the garden where a little punch is welcomed.

Cool Colors

The cool colors include blue, purple, green, and the tertiary colors in between. They are considered passive and give an impression of calm. White and pale yellow both pair well with cool colors.

Because cool colors absorb more light than they reflect, they are less noticeable from afar and tend to look smaller or disappear completely with distance. They can also look

washed out in the sun, as is the case with pastels. Cool colors work best when used up close.

White

White is the absence of color. It works particularly well in areas of your garden that are mostly enjoyed when the sun goes down. Colorful flower gardens fade at night, but white pops.

One popular sort of monochromatic garden is the "white garden." The classic White Garden in the Sissinghurst Castle Garden in England provides a beautiful example.

Perspective

Color can also be used in the garden to change perspective. Carefully using color in a certain way can make a small garden look larger.

The human eye works in a way that creates an aerial perspective—saturated, intense colors, such as a dark blue, will appear to be nearer to you. You can see an example of this when you look at a mountain range. The mountains nearest you look darker blue, while the mountains farther back become a lighter and paler blue until they almost disappear, giving the sense of depth. In your garden, using more saturated colors in one area will make those plants appear to be closer. You could select colors that range from intense purplish-blue to medium blue to pale blue, and perspective will make the paler flowers look much farther away than they actually are. So, if you have a small garden space in your backyard that you want to appear larger than it really is, this trick will help you accomplish that.

Year-Round Color

Adding color in the spring and summer is easy to do when there are so many flowers in bloom. In the fall and winter, too, color abounds in woody plants, bark, seeds, and berries. Holly, both evergreen and deciduous, adds color in my winter garden, as do early blooming daffodils, tulips, and yellow- and red-stem dogwood. Making a point to find plants that have three or more seasons of interest will engage you longer in the garden.

When you repeat colors in a garden design, they help move your eye along the border. Don't limit your color palette to just flowers. Foliage, gazing globes, and other accents can play a lively role in a garden's color scheme.

GARDENING WITH CONFIDENCE

Consider Your Light

Color is not only about personal preference—local conditions can make a big difference in the color choices that will make your garden powerful.

When I lived in London, the light was considerably different than what I was used to on the east coast of the United States. In England, hot colors looked dull and mute. Pastels dominated many of the landscapes because they worked well—brightening up the naturally dull gray light.

France was where I had to go for a hot color fix. The light was phenomenal in Paris. It's the most flattering light—to plants and people—I've ever experienced. The yellows were more vibrant, the reds magnificent. Back home, particularly where I live in Raleigh, pastels are washed away by the bright sunlight beaming down on my flowers. But hot colors can hold their own in that more intense light. It's not always a matter of what colors complement—also consider how the light will affect the color in your particular area.

The orange containers peeking out in the background bring a pop of bright color to my garden.

FENCE FOLLIES

Warm and welcoming, fences surround the property and tie the home and garden together, making the area from the front door to the fence an extension of the ground floor. The fence, acting as a barrier between your home and the hustle and bustle of daily life, provides you with privacy and protection. But fences can be so much more. A fence can also serve as your folly—a functional fence area can become something fun and whimsical, too.

Fences can convey feelings. Seeing fences along a country road conjures up the comfort of a space that is open and yet so well contained. There is just something cozy about a white picket fence. Any fence that pairs nicely with your own home's style will stir up a warm, homey feeling for all passersby.

A fence material doesn't have to dictate the style, however. A material can lend itself to various styles. Metal fencing materials aren't only for formal styles, although they are often seen surrounding formal homes.

The materials you select for your fence should complement those used in your house. A painted picket fence adds charm to a clapboard home painted the same color. A wrought iron fence adds an air of formality, echoing a home's formal style. Similarly, Craftsman-style homes should have similar style fences, or the two will not harmonize with each other.

When selecting a fence style, a good place to start narrowing down your design options is by repeating or mimicking details found elsewhere in your home's architecture. If your

This colorful garden border features soft pink roses that shine against the white fence.

porch railing has a Chippendale design, the same style will work wonderfully for a fence. If your porch railing is made of wood, using wood as your fence material is a natural choice.

Whether you have an existing fence or plan to install a fence in the future, consider planting a garden, as well. A fence is the perfect folly for any garden, an opportunity not to be missed. Fences become accents in garden designs, a wonderful backdrop for garden beds.

Setting the fence back from the curb or street allows for an area to be planted as garden in front of the fence. Add a gate to provide visitors an opportunity to pause and admire the garden as they open it and pass through.

Consider the depth of your front-of-fence garden. It could be narrow, a mere 6 inches (15.2cm), with just a fluff of greenery, such as liriope, to soften the edge. Or you could add an area just over 3 feet (1m) deep for a full-scale garden. The bed shouldn't be too deep for you to reach it for garden maintenance from just one side.

Think about adding plants for year-round interest. After all, your folly will be a focal point, as well. Layering with trees, shrubs, perennials, annuals, grasses, bulbs, and vines, and adding a mix of herbaceous and evergreen plantings will give the design enough variety to maintain interest in every season.

Fencing on the sides of the property and in the backyard offers the perfect structure to use as a backdrop to your garden plantings. You can leave your fences unpainted or paint them your favorite color to give interest and provide year-round color.

If nothing else, your fence can be a conversation starter. Your personal style will decide if the fence will match the home—or match the color of your favorite iris. The entire fence might not support such bold painting, but a dedicated corner could be your spot to get creative. Adding a fence gives opportunity for folly in the garden and freedom to express yourself.

I used this tobacco fence in my garden to cover a chain-link fence and add more of my own style.

Blend or Soften Unattractive Fencing

If your home has an unattractive galvanized chain-link fence, there are a few things you can do to keep it from being an eyesore, beyond overplanting to hide it. Painting the fence a deep forest green, nearly black, will make the fence visually disappear. Taking the harsh metal finish and softening it to a background color found in nature will let the fence blend in with the surroundings better.

Another idea is to soften the fence with a cover-up. When we moved into our current home, there was a galvanized fence along the back of the property line. To soften the fence, we attached panels of reed fencing. These can be bought either online or at garden centers and big box stores for the purpose of covering an eyesore without having to invest much money. They are easy and fast to install: a panel can go up in less than half an hour. They are not a permanent solution, but they are long-lasting. My current reed fence panels have been in place for 10 years and are just starting to show some wear.

CREATING A FOCAL POINT

As you walk down a garden path, your senses are heightened and delighted. With a continual swath of beautiful plants, your eye takes in so much beauty, moving from flower to flower and from one vignette to another. Then your eyes come to rest on a particular item in the garden—a focal point—giving your senses a place to rest and feel all that joy. Adding a focal point helps register that elation in the heart.

A focal point can be a fountain, a perfectly placed birdhouse, or a piece of garden art. It can be anything, really, including specimen plants, as long as it's something eye-catching enough to add emphasis to the garden. A focal point is the "sigh spot" for wandering eyes to rest and bring the full garden into focus.

When selecting a focal point, keep in mind that it is meant to become the center of visual attention along a line of sight—from a path, open space, broad border, or other vista—offering the viewer something to concentrate on. Without this, a relationship among the elements will not be established, and you will lose the attention of the viewer.

The focal point should also stay within your garden style theme. Formal elements, such as an obelisk, work well in formal gardens. Rustic birdhouses and birdbaths work well in cottage gardens.

Larger gardens or gardens with many rooms, large or small, may have more than one focal point. Consider adding focal points in many areas of the garden, being careful not to add more than one in a single location. Ideally,

These two colorful pots pull the visitor's focus.

when someone is standing in the line of sight, only one focal point should be visible at a time. As a person moves around the garden, the previous focal point will fade as other focal points present themselves.

Here are some suggestions for focal points to add to your garden:

- A large border of green can be brought to life with a focal point. A red, feathery Japanese maple planted among evergreens will draw the eye in for a rest before moving on.
- Smaller spaces can have one unique plant that grabs the attention and jazzes up the space—for example, a small-scale weeping Japanese maple, the orange leaves of cannas, or the sinuous lines of a weeping blue atlas cedar.
- Running water is often heard before it is seen. This prepares us for joys that await nearby. In listening, we know as we journey through a garden that something

GARDENING WITH CONFIDENCE

The Perfect Position

Every good garden design has at least one dominating focal point. Whether it's in the form of an urn, a plant, or art, a well-placed focal point can make or break a garden's emotional appeal. A large decorative in the middle of a garden bed, for example, can completely make the garden, adding height, interest, and intrigue.

Focal points don't need to be elaborate concoctions to grab someone's attention; a simple, perfectly positioned item will let the eye relax and enjoy before moving on.

A pond always acts as a natural focal point.

will present itself. No matter where a fountain is placed, it will naturally become a focal point. It will also become a hub for the wildlife it attracts.

- Set a statue front and center or have it whispering for attention from among the flowers and foliage. Statues demand attention and add emphasis to other features, such as a pool or doorway.
- Adding a single boulder or a series of boulders to a garden border creates drama and serves as a focal

point. Boulders also serve as a backdrop to complement plantings within a border. If you live in an already rocky area, boulders will offer a natural alternative for focal points.

As you focus on improving your garden display, consider where you might add a focal point for year-round enjoyment. A focal point will break up an expanse of plants and draw the eye in. From there, your garden will reveal itself.

CHAPTER 21

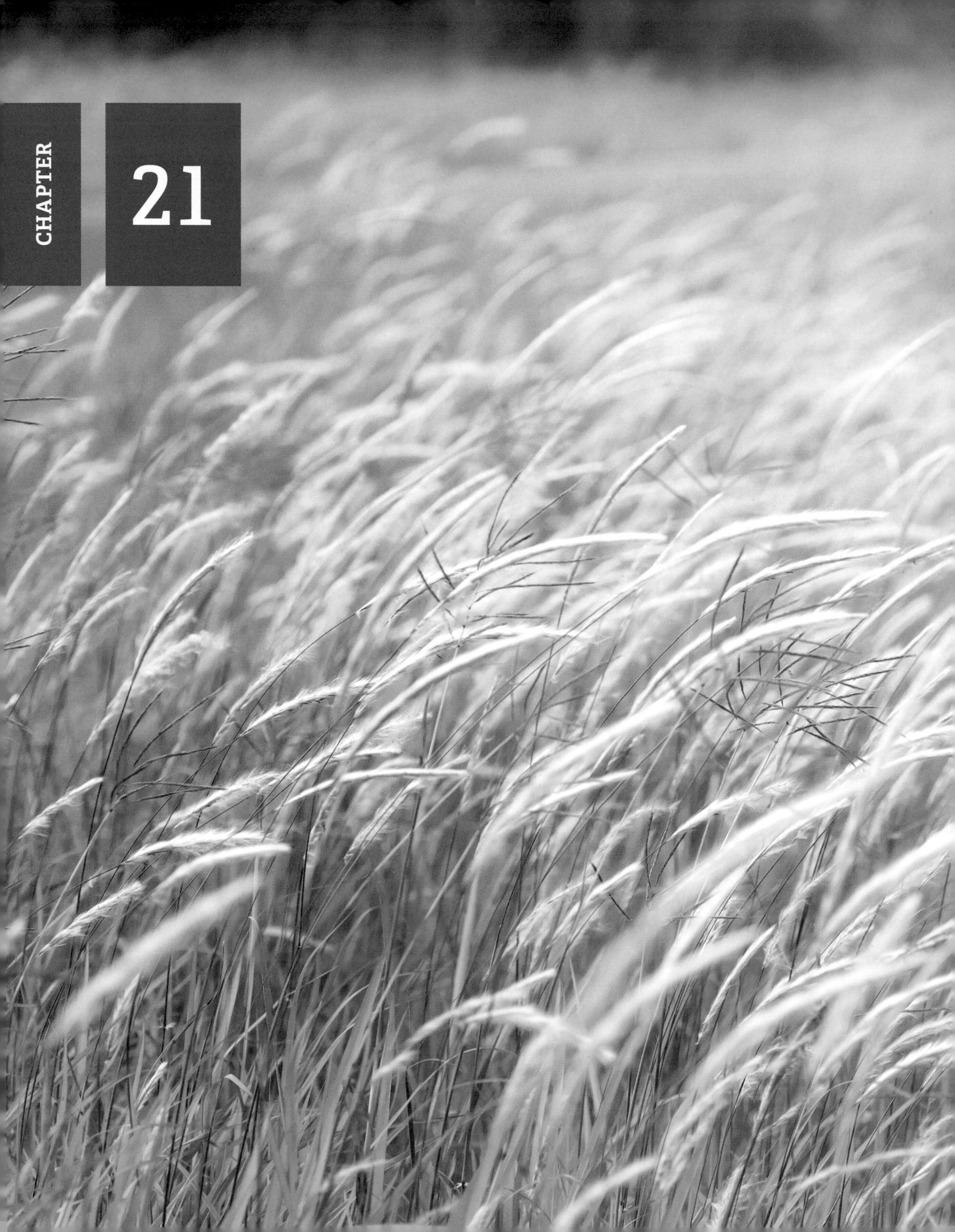

MOVEMENT IN THE GARDEN

Wind blowing, water flowing, grasses swaying, children playing—movement brings a garden to life.

It seems unimaginable for a garden to be still. Do you find yourself looking from the corner of your eye at a twitching leaf, or do you look toward a sound made by the wind blowing through some grasses? Movement engages you in the garden. It can be introduced in so many ways, such as through plants, water features, or art. More than likely, your own garden already holds a number of movement-makers that are just waiting to be discovered.

Certain trees keep their leaves throughout the winter. White oak trees will hold on to their leaves, which turn brown and dry in winter, until new spring growth pushes out the old. As the wind rises, the rustling leaves draw the eye upward. Certain shrubs also hold their leaves when dormant, such the spice bush (*Lindera glauca*). Their dried, spice-colored leaves provide a rattle in the wind during the wintertime.

As water flows, its movement (and sound) attracts the gardener and wildlife, alike. From four-tiered fountains and recirculating ponds to gurgling urns with barely enough flow to coat the sides, moving water will entice birds and other wildlife to sip or dip. The sound of moving water also buffers ambient noise, creating a focal point to be enjoyed most of the year. Watching fish move through the water is calming and cathartic. Fish move left, move right, and circle

Tall grass adds natural movement.

around. They wiggle and twist, looking for bites to eat and making sure all is well in their watery world. During fish feeding times, the fish are fun to watch as they scurry into position, breaking the water as they grab little nibbles.

Grasses, with their flexibility, add movement to the garden in all seasons. Swaying in the wind, the grasses' bending acts like an anemometer measuring for speed—the stronger the wind, the more the bend. Perennial *Calamagrostis × acutiflora* 'Karl Foerster' stands upright and erect until the breeze begins. *Muhlenbergia capillaries* colors up pink in the fall, then fades to tan for the winter months. Native switch grass, *Panicum virgatum* 'Shenandoah', can grow up to 4 feet (1.2m) tall, adding nice red tones in the summer and growing darker burgundy as the fall progresses. In the winter, 'Shenandoah' is blond and bold, ready to bend in the slightest breeze.

One of your garden's greatest movement-makers could very well come in the form of children at play. They can

GARDENING WITH CONFIDENCE

Add Variety

Waving flags, whirligigs, and wagging dogs—all are great ways to add movement to your garden. Carry your style with these movement-makers. From flying the American flag to casually hanging a seasonal flag near the mailbox, watching movement in the garden brings your mind to attention. Movement will engage you. Surprise yourself by placing movement-makers in an area of the garden to catch the corner of your eye. Chimes hanging from a tree or mirrored ornaments that sparkle in the wind as the sun's rays catch in the reflection—you should bring your own style to the garden with what moves you.

For my garden, I've added various kinds of movement, some that are constant but mostly those that are fleeting. The water in the fountain flows as a constant, with the water pouring from one tier to the next. It's predictable and soothing. The movement of a butterfly passing is fleeting. The kids add fleeting movements—as they run and play. The movement of the wind never stops intriguing me. My most memorable movement-makers have the greatest effect on those days when, seemingly out of nowhere, Earth's breath moves leaves, sways grasses, and pushes chimes to make melodic garden sounds.

Garden visitors like hummingbirds bring lots of entertaining movement!

bring life to a garden in a way with which little else can compare. From chasing fireflies to playing tag to climbing trees, kids delight in roaming outdoors and can infuse your whole yard with motion.

Place your favorite movement-makers where they can best be observed. A fountain might be seen from the front window or in your courtyard where you can sit for some quiet solitude. Think about placing nectar-rich plants near the back porch so you can watch the pollinators come and go. Observing a hummingbird pause in mid-air before deciding which flower to visit next will bring you endless delight. You'll be grateful to see carefully placed grasses along the driveway, bending hello to welcome you home.

Watching your world in motion adds another level of joy and fascination to the garden. If none of these ideas suit you, just add a whirligig at the front door, and you will be ready to witness wind in motion.

SOUND

As I walk through the garden in winter, I hear a breeze coming before I feel it brush my face. The pin oak, still in its infancy at a mere 20 years old, holds its leaves through the winter. It is brown and nondescript until the wind blows, and then a wonderful sound occurs. Looking up, I see the leaves shimmering like a hula skirt, making me feel like I could shimmy a bit myself. As I listen, all around me the garden has become a symphony of sounds.

Sound in the garden is often overlooked as a garden design element. I'm not talking about boom box sound, although there is a time and place for music in the garden. I'm talking about the sound of nature. The leaves, birds, bees, bugs, bats, and even decorative ornaments that bring life to a silent spot. Frogs croaking, insect wings vibrating, cicadas buzzing—these sounds can conjure up memories and instill curiosity. Billowing grasses bend in the wind, causing a quaking between their blades. Seeds rattle in the rustle of a breeze, giving you the pleasure of hearing their call, a dinner bell for seed-eating songbirds.

Complete silence in nature is a fearful thing—we think of it as a harbinger of storms and tornados. Perhaps the crickets can be deafening during the summer when the windows are open and you are trying to sleep. But not hearing any sound at all, in reality, is much worse. Happy are the sounds of nature.

Water provides one of my favorite garden sounds. Whether it's a recirculating fountain muting the ambient noise of nearby traffic or

A robin splashes around in the birdbath.

a pond fully stocked with fish splashing and drawing you over to investigate—the sound of moving water is at the same time peaceful and full of life.

Water will also invite wildlife and its noises to your garden. A water feature will attract amphibians, which need water for part of their life cycle and for protection. You will delight in the sounds of frogs and toads, happily croaking until you approach on your evening walk and they splash into the water. They not only provide you with sound pleasure, they also diminish the annoying sound of the approaching mosquito (which is also about to become a frog's nighttime nosh).

A garden abuzz with bugs and insects adds yet another layer to your garden symphony. Try attracting pollinators for reasons beyond pollination—for the pure pleasure of the sounds they bring, such as the sound of busy bees working the flowers in the beds out back.

Wildlife brings so much more than sound to the garden. Animal and insect interaction in the garden is part of what keeps your garden in nature's balance. Many birds in the garden will feed on insects and reward you with song. Attracting birds is easy to do and part of the fun of building a garden. Include plants that will provide food and protection, as well as nesting material. The more sustainable the garden, the

GARDENING WITH CONFIDENCE

Chaos and Calm

For better or worse, if I'm reading on a Saturday afternoon in a comfortable location, listening to the kids play outside, I will slip into the nap position. I don't have the luxury to plan for a nap, but when the melodic sounds of kids playing in the garden last for too long, I'm soothed to sleep.

Sound in the garden is one of my greatest joys. Whether it's from the birds chirping, bees buzzing, children keeping score, or just the sounds the wind brings, sound comforts me. And when many sounds blend together, chaos becomes calm, resting the soul.

Wind chimes bring a calming, peaceful sound to an outdoor space.

more likely birds that don't migrate will call your garden home year-round. A simple water source, such as a birdbath, will provide the birds a necessity and bring you joy as you watch and hear the birds coming close for a sip or a dip.

One of my favorite sounds in the garden is one I hear when I travel down the gravel path on the south side of my house. I hear the birds take flight from my approaching footsteps crunching on the gravel path. The sound of the birds taking flight never ceases to delight my senses. As the birds depart, a smile always forms on my lips.

Though not a part of nature, chimes can be charming as the wind sways them. The size of the chime and the material they are made of affects the sound. Large metal chimes cause deep melodic sounds, while tiny treasures will sound like a chuckwagon dinner bell. Bamboo provides a muted sound, while shells cause a clatter. It's a personal preference—in all cases, the chimes will alert the gardener, even inside the house, to changes in the wind outside.

We people add sound as we journey through the garden, too, whether crunching on gravel or brushing against languid plantings that soften the edges along the paths. When we walk the garden, we contribute to the life of the garden.

PRIVACY

Seasonal splendor draws us outside to enjoy time with our families or just to be alone in the garden. When venturing outside, do you often come face to face with a neighbor seeking the same? Even if you have great neighbors, most of us want to have some private time. Privacy can provide a comforting sense of seclusion and security. While we are social creatures, there are times we want to be alone in the garden—or at least, feel alone without being open for inspection.

Privacy is becoming increasingly precious. When creating some for yourself, go beyond fencing. Add privacy in a variety of sizes, textures, and colors by using plants, including trees, shrubs, perennials, and even vines. This will not only provide privacy, it will also add interest and attract more wildlife.

The first place to start is to evaluate your goals for privacy. Are you trying to create a sense of enclosure? Do you want to hide the driveway or block the view of your neighbor's deck or patio? Do you need privacy year-round or just during specific times? Plan and plant for privacy based on your specific needs.

Careful evaluation of the landscape will help you identify where you want to place plants for privacy. This will help you see whether or not a complete barrier is necessary in a particular area. While complete enclosure can be nice, it may be that all you really need is to block a bit of your neighbor's window. If that is the case, just a few well-placed plants—or perhaps even just one shrub—will be enough, creating privacy when and where it's needed most.

A gate door in a lush hedge can create a secret garden hideaway.

It's also a good idea to know how your privacy screening works. Is it all built on your neighbor's property? If so, you may want to consider adding a privacy barrier on your side, as well. You never know if your neighbor or the next owner will keep those plants. What may be important privacy to you may only be a hedgerow to them.

Oftentimes only seasonal privacy is needed for blocking the view of a neighbor or a shed. Maybe you enjoy spending the most time in your garden for spring teas, summer cocktails, or fall cookouts; select tall plants that will peak during the

seasons you are most likely to be outdoors, allowing you to benefit from the privacy they provide as well as their beauty. Year-round privacy may not be needed or desired. Sometimes openness can be useful as well, such as allowing in more light during the winter.

Think about using plants to create private areas around your garden, as well. A long, single-species hedgerow can create a garden room, becoming a backdrop for a planting plan. With the hedgerow providing privacy and serving as a wall, a garden could be started from there, with the privacy

GARDENING WITH CONFIDENCE

Privacy with Personality

Whether you add a fence, hedgerow, or single shrub to block a view, creating privacy is another opportunity to add your own personal touches. Break up a long row of identical hedges with a cute birdhouse or feeder or another type of tall vertical garden accent.

Containers in front of the hedgerow can change the rhythm of the space, at the same time allowing you to personalize the space. A privacy backdrop, whether it is created with fencing or plants, can also be embellished with a birdbath, bench, or garden art, giving you a chance to express more of your style.

It's important to enjoy quiet moments for yourself.

hedge as the backdrop. During the garden bed's peak, the privacy hedgerow will disappear. As the front garden display dies back in the off-season, the hedgerow takes center stage again.

Keep in mind that diversity of plant species will be good insurance against widespread pest damage. Having a variety of plants will lessen the wait period should one shrub in a row of shrubs be lost. Your barrier will be presentable while you wait for the new plant to catch up to the rest.

As an added bonus for planting a privacy buffer, you're also providing cover and habitat for wildlife to raise young. With a selection of plantings that provide fruit, such as hollies, you also provide food. The sounds of life emanating from a hedgerow can be reason enough for adding privacy plantings.

With a good design, your privacy screen can serve multiple purposes. It will not only give you the private space you desire but will also become a part of your garden to admire and enjoy.

GARDEN SEATING

As I pull into the driveway of an old friend, I look fondly at the welcoming bench in her front yard. Although I've never seen her sit on it, over the years the bench has held her purse, her groceries, and me. It is often the place I choose to wait for her if I arrive to pick her up for an afternoon outing before she is ready; more than just a place to sit, it affords me the opportunity to enjoy her garden from a different perspective.

Outdoor seating can be a cheerful, inviting touch that also provides functionality. A bench like my friend's, for example, becomes a focal point that adds to the home's curb appeal, makes for a handy place to gather goods, and, of course, is a place to sit a spell, either coming or going. When a table and chairs are a part of your garden décor, you can take advantage of outdoor seating by dining al fresco. In general, seating outside can be placed anywhere a respite might be welcome. With the right consideration, you can plan places to sit in your garden that will both look attractive and serve as a place from which you can admire the view.

Your available space will help define your placement choices. Areas that are private are good places to consider adding garden seats. Review the different parts of your garden and ask yourself what seating areas you can provide and how many people they can hold. Small, intimate areas are perfect for a secluded retreat. The large, more open spaces are ideal for seasonal soirees. Most people will gravitate to seats that offer a sense of security.

Relaxation areas are key!

Placing a bench or a pair of chairs against the side of a building, fence, or hedge will give the seating a cozy and inviting feel.

When placing seating in the garden, make the transition seamless by adding plantings to soften the edges. Surround the seats with containers or put them under a tree. Make sure the seating is accessible and welcoming. Create your resting place next to fragrant plants or

in areas with seasonal colors. Relate the bench to its surroundings, echoing your home's style and color, for example, a white painted bench is the perfect choice for a home with white trim and a white picket fence. The farther your seats are from your house, the less true you need to stay to your home's style.

Sitting changes a person's perspective. Every view will be looked at with different eyes at a lower level. Arrange the

GARDENING WITH CONFIDENCE

Change Your Perspective

In my early days of gardening, I only added a bench or chair as an accent and in the off-chance I might actually sit there. For that reason alone, seating is worth adding to the garden setting. But as my garden matured, and I along with it, those seats became something to explore. Now you will find me sitting in any of the eight seating areas (not counting the covered porch). My seats range from a solitary chair to an antique metal glider for a respite or a change in perspective. It's amazing how different the garden looks when you are sitting instead of standing.

Benches take on a special atmosphere when surrounded with beautiful, brilliant flowers.

seating so there is something interesting to look at or place your seating off in the distance to serve as a destination. This destination could be the end of a journey around the garden, or a place to pause and enjoy the fruits of your labor.

The hectic pace of everyday life slows when you are in a garden. Taking time to leave your day behind is easier when your favorite chair is actually in the backyard. Sit for a moment to listen to the sounds of the garden abuzz with

life or to watch the blooms in the setting sun. Whether it is a simple bench that beckons you for a rest or a pair of chairs comfortably arranged in a garden bed, outdoor seating allows you time amongst the flowers to relax alone or with a friend.

Well-placed seating serves multiple purposes, making it the perfect accent to the garden—even if, as a busy gardener, you never have time to sit.

ACCENTING YOUR GARDEN WITH ART

Rounding a curved path, I spy a splash of blue color that piques my interest. Is it a flower or a glimmer of garden art? Either way, my excitement swells, but deep down, I'm hoping to see a perfectly placed piece of garden art.

Art can beautifully accent any garden and give the gardener another way to showcase their individuality. When thoughtfully selected and purposefully placed, it can bring the garden to a brilliant new level. Beware the danger of overdoing it, though, and letting your garden become something reminiscent of a scrap yard.

For a long time, I had an affinity for a particular whimsical garden accent—bunnies, bunnies, and more bunnies. Even then, I wondered why I was so enamored with concrete bunnies, when, at the same time, I was showing so much disdain for the real ones nibbling to nubs my cherished plantings.

Today, I've moved beyond bunnies. I want more than cute concrete critters in my garden. I want art.

For many years, I visited gardens that had been included on the Garden Conservancy's Open Days tour. I studied these gardens and wondered—what made them a cut above? In every case, the designs, including the garden art, were perfect in scale and had a distinct sense of place. Each piece of art had been positioned to be viewed from multiple angles. At no time was one piece of art competing with another. Each piece was placed to be the focal point, whether

One of the few bunny sculptures I've kept in the garden.

You can use a piece of art in the garden to echo and complement plant colors and textures.

as a bold, stand-alone feature or one tucked away, whispering for attention among the flowers and foliage.

While the art's quality is certainly important, placement is every bit as crucial. Add art in areas where plants are difficult to grow, such as a soggy spot, or on top of stumps, which provide the perfect spots for placing decorative containers. Art can also be used to add interest to borders and paths, creating small stops on the path so that the journey seems longer than it actually is.

The placement of your garden art will have more impact than the quality of the piece. Your garden art should have a sense of place. You will know if it looks right when you see it; there is no design formula to tell you how it's done (I can only present suggestions here). The perfect placement may not be your originally planned location. Move the art around to find the location for which it is best suited. If the supporting plants near your art lose their foliage in winter, your garden art may need to be stored until the foliage returns. This is OK; consider it part of your annual maintenance.

At one point looking around my own garden, I realized I had very few pieces that were actually made

by hand. Most of the pieces I had were accents, not art. I define art as something that has been made with a beating heart, while accents tend to be more mass-produced resin or concrete critters. I also had far too many of them.

Fortunately, I had some true garden art, too. Each of these pieces was perfectly placed. However, I had junked up the scene with lesser quality pieces, making the view cluttered. As I mentioned in chapter 7 (beginning on page 33), I edited my garden art and accent placement. I examined each piece and evaluated it for its merit. My requirement was simple—it had to be handmade. I also thought it had merit if it was sentimental or special in some other way. In any case, the pieces that made the cut were placed back in the garden with much more consideration.

In the end, I find that if a piece of garden art is handmade, it is of more value to me. This is the focus of my garden art, and I use this rule to keep the clutter at bay.

Garden art is something very personal, and it will truly reflect your personality and style, making a garden your own.

GARDENING WITH CONFIDENCE

Invest in Art You Truly Love

I never thought I could part with the kind of money that good garden art would cost. Then I realized I had already spent enough on lesser accents that could have been saved for a single, very special piece. I would spend $35 on an accent, and since the price was so right, over time I would add another and another. Soon, I had 10 pieces at $35 apiece. Instead, I could have spent $350 on a single artwork that blended better with my garden.

ARBORS

You round a corner and there, reaching for the sky, a flower-filled arbor frames a lovely view. An arbor serves as a portal into a garden room, a transition point to tell a visitor it's time to pause, to change perspective. Training vines to cover the arbor brings garden life to another dimension. There are so many reasons to want to find the perfect spot in your garden to add an arbor.

Arbors have the ability to set a mood. Romantic, rustic, formal, Asian, European, or cottage-style—an arbor knows no architectural boundaries. The connection between house and garden is extended when the style of the arbor matches the home. Repeating interesting architectural details found on the house, such as the porch railing pattern, gable's pitch, color, or even a pattern found in the window mullions, will help add continuity between the house and the garden.

Arbors come in all shapes and sizes to match any desired effect. Skinny arbors, just deep enough to adequately stabilize themselves and the plants they support, are common. An arbor deep enough for seating can become a child's play area for hosting other children or a teddy bear's picnic. Arbor seats can also be a special place for quiet repose.

Very deep arbor designs can serve as vine-covered eating areas for al fresco dining—just saying the words conjures up a longing to eat

This arbor is the perfect structure for showcasing bright purple clematis in full bloom.

outside on a warm summer evening. Bring out your best china and crystal to toast with friends the glory that only outdoor dining can bring.

Wood, metal, and even old tree branches can be fashioned into arbors. However, ready-built arbors are plentiful. You'll find them at flea markets, antique stores, garden centers, and home improvement stores.

Any garden, large or small, has space for at least one arbor (and maybe more). Analyze your property to find where you can divide areas of the yard to make more of your space. This is an idea known as "multiplication by division"—expanding the space by dividing the area into smaller sections. Magically, the garden seems larger when you sequester parts of it into new sites.

To see where you can add an arbor to your garden, go on a walking tour of your property. Survey it from as many vantage points as possible: from the back looking toward the house, from the corners of the property, or even from the middle of the open spaces in the backyard or side yards.

GARDENING WITH CONFIDENCE

Choose Plants That Work with Your Life

The arbor in my garden is in a very traditional place—on the north side of the property and used to access the back garden. I chose this spot to add an arbor since it was at a transition point where the side of the house ended and the backyard began.

The arbor is draped with a semievergreen (for us in Zone 7b, at least) vine called a crossvine (*Bignonia capreolata*, 'Tangerine Beauty'). A crossvine is an aggressive vine that requires pruning to keep the arbor itself from looking like a shapeless arch. But since I garden with confidence, this is not a problem for me. An annual pruning and thinning is all it needs.

Pick your battles with nature. If a plant gives me more in return than the maintenance it requires, then that's good enough for me. If the vine needed my attention on a monthly basis, I would have replaced it long ago. We all know our tolerance and what is acceptable. Find what works for you.

This garden arbor leads to a quaint forest path.

Your arbor can become the doorway to a garden room if you add low fence sections or a hedge buffer to create walls. Arbors also direct foot traffic through the garden, standing tall and enticing you to come within. Adding paths and walls with your arbor creates transition points or separate rooms. Passing through the arbor transforms the space and also the mood of the viewer, who feels as if they're embarking on an adventure.

Most arbors stand 8 to 10 feet (2.4 to 3.1m) tall. This gives sufficient clearance to walk under, even when flowering vines drip with nectar and scent. This height also makes pruning vines when needed more manageable. Vining plants can be used alone. You can train an American wisteria over the arbor or pair combinations of plants, like the classic duo of clematis and rose. Top your arbor with twinkling lights, providing illumination for you and the garden fairies alike as you make a welcome journey into the evening garden.

COVERED PORCHES

On nights when I can't sleep, you'll find me changing my perspective out back in the shelter of my covered porch. A covered porch is an extension of the home into the garden, a bridge between house and garden. Protected from rain but open to gentle breezes, a covered porch is a place you don't know how much you need until you've built it.

In modern times, the American front porch is a uniquely original architectural style, and we have no clear understanding of how it evolved. Some historians believe it stemmed from Europeans, who, although they didn't bring the style from their homelands, added the space to their homes to be a semi-indoor escape from the heat. Others believe it was brought over with the Africans as part of their traditional architectural style. In either case, the front porch has become universally recognized as an American iconic architectural style.

In the 1800s and early 1900s, front porches were a place to sit out and socialize with neighbors walking by or slowing down in their carriages. As homes became more suburban, the social aspect of the front porch was lost. The newer porches were built to be decorative rather than functional, as the American way of life moved into the backyard. Cookouts, touch football, playing croquet—entertainments for a sunny day—were performed out back. As such, backyard patios and decks became the new American gathering spots.

Our home had a decorative front porch and a deck out back that we used when enjoying

Covered porches are a good place to wind down.

the main garden. We sought shelter from the sun with a market umbrella resting on the wooden deck. We used the space often, but rain would move us inside. After living in our house for 10 years, we decided to build a covered porch in the backyard. Our purpose was to extend our time outside. If the weather turned bad, we could find refuge from the storm without going indoors entirely. We soon realized the back porch was more than shelter. It was an extension of our home. The covered porch enlarged the space without changing the footprint.

To find the right size for your own porch, first determine how you will use the space. When creating a covered porch, you don't want it to be too small—you'll feel cramped and uncomfortable. If the porch is too big, you could feel overwhelmed, and the space won't feel intimate enough. Will the porch be a social place or a private retreat? In our case, we wanted a place for the kids to play, for friends to gather, and for a quiet cup of coffee to welcome the morning light. We wanted it to be both a private oasis and a place to entertain.

There are some useful numbers to know when designing your porch or for understanding how to modify your existing space to allow for certain needs. For overall space, allow 4 square feet (1.2m²) for each person who is likely to join you on the porch. For a dining area, allocate a perimeter of 3 square feet (91.4cm²) of open space around each table setting. This will allow for comfortable circulation around the dining table.

Just as you accent your home's interior, so too will you want to accent your covered porch with container gardens, ornaments, and surfaces for food or drink. Good lighting is a must. Our porch has floodlights pouring light along the nearby garden, as well as recessed can lights that can be dimmed as desired. There are ceiling fans to cool us in the summer and to push the mosquitoes away. Music can stream through at those times when music is essential. Comfortable furniture keeps our friends lingering with us.

When my nocturnal forays take me to the covered porch, a whole new world comes to life. For those of you who have lost touch with your nocturnal side, take a peek outside to see what awaits you at night when other people are asleep and the wildlife comes out to roam.

A covered porch is an extension of the home's interior, allowing you to expand your home into a protected transition place to welcome your guests to the garden. It's the perfect place to rest and enjoy a cold drink in summer or a hot one in winter after time spent working or walking in the garden.

This covered porch features a gorgeous daybed and eclectic accents that create a comfortable space.

To Screen or Not to Screen

Here in the South, homeowners often steer clear of having a covered porch. A screened-in porch is more to their liking because it deters insects, such as mosquitoes and flies. My covered porch is unscreened. I chose not to have it screened to better view the garden. But when food comes out, so do these uninvited guests. Flies can be controlled with cute plate covers, but we found it's best to fill the plates inside and then bring them out into the garden, leaving the serving dishes inside. A single person can easily monitor a single plate. Flies are not a reason to eat inside; we just manage our individual plates and enjoy being outside.

With regard to mosquitoes, ceiling fans work well—the moving air keeps the mosquitoes from being able to land. Besides, nothing says summer like the movement of air outside on an arid day or witnessing the freshness of an afternoon rain under the protection of a covered porch.

GARDEN BED EDGING

Curved beds with echoing color and dazzling rhythm often fall short on presence when they are frayed at the edges. Freshening up the edges of a garden bed is like adding the perfect pair of earrings to your favorite little black dress.

Garden bed edging can be as simple as shifting from turf to hardscape materials, temporarily or permanently, to tidy up an edge. The addition of edging is often overlooked, but it adds value to the overall garden design. Without a crisp transition, a garden bed can look unfinished. Even a country garden, where a casual aloofness reigns, benefits from a finished edge.

Adding an edge can help contain the patio paving material and serves to visually unify other landscape and architectural features. The area where a bed ends and turf begins needs a transition for aesthetic reasons, and it performs a function, as well. A bed's edge helps keep your garden tidy while holding back soil, defining lines, keeping mulch from migrating into the lawn, and preventing weeds from creeping into the bed.

Many edge types can be added in an afternoon. Others, such as brick or boulders, may require a weekend or longer to complete. The simplest and easiest edge to create is a V-notch made with a flat-bladed spade into the abutting turf. Other types of bed edges include brick, bender board, river stones, metal, and wood. The edging you choose should complement the style of the garden and the home, as well as your budget. Keep

Rocks can be great natural garden bed edging.

in mind that spending more doesn't necessarily give you a better bed edge. V-notch edges are the cheapest to install, and they are often found edging gardens at the very formal, stately homes that shelter owners with deep pockets.

Most of my beds are edged with simple V-notched edges. The V-notched edge responds well to an edge trimmer, keeping the lines crisp. Each year, right before I mulch, I re-dig the lines, taking the dirt along the edge and heaping it about 6 inches (15.2cm) back, tapering toward the freshly dug area. The area then gets a top-dressing of mulch.

Brick makes a lovely edge. I'm partial to brick-lined edges since my home in London had an oval-shaped garden with a brick-lined edge. It was simply perfect. Brick adds a classic look to any garden setting. If you are only edging your garden, mortar isn't even needed.

Bender board offers an easy solution to adding sinuous curves to the garden bed. Today's bender board is composed of recycled plastic in colors to match your garden decor.

Edging and Path Inspiration

When I lived in London during graduate school, I learned a lot about gardening. One of my favorite takeaways was that every home had a "garden." A yard was the word used to refer to the grounds of an industrial or commercial site, but every home's land was referred to as a garden.

The garden in the home I rented for three years had an oval path circling the back of a long, narrow garden space. The center of the oval was grass, with informal beds all around. Given the oval shape, the corners of the garden were deeper and supported larger plants, with ornamental trees anchoring the lot. Even though it wasn't what I think of as a lush garden, it had perfect proportions and enough going on. You wanted to be in the garden without feeling like you needed to do anything there except enjoy the moment.

The oval shape was enforced with a path that also served as edging. The path was 18 inches (45.7cm) wide and made of brick. I would walk out the back door and begin a journey at the path, slowly making my way around the entire garden. This little patch of garden, a mere 50 feet (15.2m) wide by 100 feet (30.5m) deep, had more impact on my gardening style than any other garden. Its simplicity of design left an imprint on my aesthetic style. While I haven't invested the time or money to put such edging in my garden, my design was created to someday support one. It will be the final touch, a cherry on top of my sundae, something I will use and value each and every day.

Metal edging works well in modern gardens spaces.

Using locally sourced stones or rocks gives your garden edge a natural look. You might find some useful stone in your garden or get it from a friend. Like most things, skill is needed when trying to mimic nature. First, find the best face of the stone, and then place the stone so that side is the most visible. Also, burying the stone 1 to 2 inches (2.5 to 5.1cm) will give it a more natural look.

Metal edging has long been in vogue in botanical gardens and commercial settings. A new trend is also emerging, where slick designers are using metal as their muse. It's a trend I like. Creating crisp, clean lines, metal complements modern designs as well as classical.

Common uses of wood range from branches placed along the lines of a bed's edge to rustic timbers—or to manufactured landscape timbers. Wood is inexpensive and easy to install.

Too often, bed edges are neglected. But with simple installation and a little maintenance, bad bed edges can be a thing of the past.

CHAPTER 29

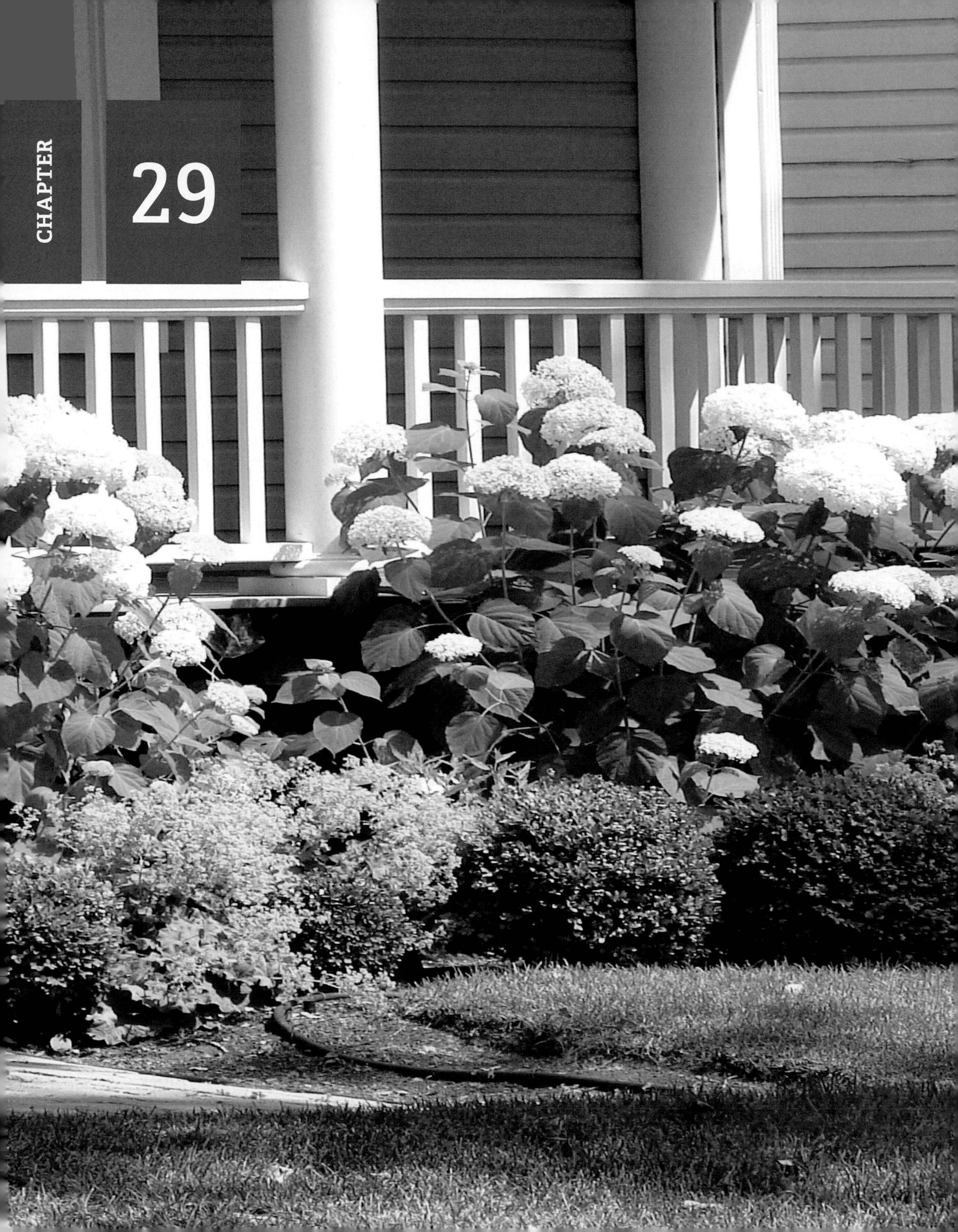

FOUNDATION PLANTINGS

Americans have long embraced a tight row of foundation plantings in the front yard. Traditionally, such plantings hid the foundation of the home, which was often made with materials different from, and often less aesthetically pleasing than, the main part of the house.

Foundation plantings originated in Victorian times, popularized by landscape architects Andrew Jackson Downing and Frederick Law Olmsted. Their use of mass plantings, like those used in designing New York City's Central Park, were emulated in home landscapes. After World War II, foundation planting schemes followed homeowners from the cities to the suburbs. Many homeowners hold fast to these older designs and plant selections, but today some homeowners are breaking free of Victorian holdovers. The typical row of foundation plants in predictable geometric forms will hopefully soon become a thing of the past, as homeowners look for more diversity, less maintenance, and more environmentally friendly plantings.

Even so, too often there still lingers a lack of creativity and poor planning in foundation gardens, with improperly selected plants hiding windows, covering air vents, and blocking crawl space access. Improper plant selection and positioning also can affect the integrity of your structure with invading root systems that retain too much moisture, attracting termites. However, having no plants has limited appeal.

Look to your home's foundation as a place where you can create a garden that will

Hydrangeas can make for lovely foundation plantings.

Foundation plantings create a warm, pleasant
feeling for homeowners and guests.

that retain too much moisture, attracting termites. However, having no plants has limited appeal.

Look to your home's foundation as a place where you can create a garden that will bring you joy as an extension of the home. Make your foundation the beginning of your landscape plan, not the end of it. A well-designed foundation plan visually anchors the house to the surrounding gardens and complements the architectural features of the home.

Let your home's style dictate your garden's style. A formal, balanced home with a center door and an equal number of windows on each side calls out for a symmetrical design. This doesn't mean each side has to mirror the other, but each side should be visually balanced with equal weight and height. An asymmetrical, informal home with unbalanced sides can support an asymmetrical design. Study the style of your home and chose plantings that tie into the architectural lines. For example, tall, narrow trees draw attention to the height of a house by accentuating vertical elements, such as columns and chimneys.

Planting your foundation in proportion to the size of your home puts your garden in scale with the house. Check each plant's tag for information on its mature height and width, and plan for its fullest possibilities. This will help eliminate future problems from overcrowding and avoid creating a sense of confinement.

Don't Play It Safe!

During the Christmas holidays, I know people who like to drive around the neighborhood to see the colorful decorations. I'm the same way with gardens—in particular, foundation plantings. I'm curious to see what my neighbors are doing with their corner choices, transitional areas from the house to the grass, and areas around the steps. Most are pleasing enough, but there are precious few who give me reason to stare.

Most homeowners play it safe with foundation plantings, following some unwritten formula. Rarely do you see flowers in bloom—and not just perennial flowers, but flowers from trees and shrubs are lacking, too. When I talked with designers and gardeners, I learned that the lack of flowers in foundation plantings is due, for the most part, to homeowners wanting to play it safe out front. In the South, it is a long-held tradition that no flowers should be in the front garden.

Live a little! Color up where it counts so that people are cheered as they walk the path to your front door. My only caution is to choose your color wisely. When colors clash, it can be catastrophic. Choose colors that complement your home and do not clash with the stone, brick, clapboard, or paint. Bad plant choices are a common problem. But be brave—don't let this keep you from adding blooming flowers to the foundation out front.

My front beds include flowers during all seasons, moving from the winter-blooming shrub winter Daphne (*Daphne odora*), to the spring-blooming shrub gardenia, to the 7 feet (2.1m) annual sulfur cosmos (*Cosmos sulphureus*), blooming all summer, and ending the year with the perennial coreopsis 'Redshift'. Seeing something in bloom each time I enter the front door, to me, says "welcome home."

Grade the soil closest to the house so that it channels water away from the foundation. It's a good idea to fill a 12-inch (30.5cm) space around the perimeter of your home with crushed gravel or stone to keep moisture, mulch, plants, and pests at bay. It's also best to maintain a working space of at least 3 feet (91.4cm) between the outermost branches of plantings and the sides of the home.

Evergreens can provide year-round interest, but including deciduous plantings for color, texture, and structure will add pleasing changes throughout the seasons that you can joyfully experience with each pass through your front door. Staggering the bloom times and selecting plants that echo the colors found in the home's exterior components (such as brick, paint, and stone on the facade) will add rhythm to the appearance of both the home and garden.

Foundation plantings finish off the welcoming feeling that is first established with your "curb appeal." Together, these ideas will let the front areas of your home make a lasting impression on old friends and newcomers alike.

WATER—FOUNTAINS AND PONDS

Perhaps it's ironic that I have a water-wise garden design, a design in which plants need little watering once they are established—and yet, I believe adding a water feature was one of the most important aspects of my garden design. The use of water goes beyond utilitarian concerns, such as adding water for wildlife to drink and bathe in (or even reproduce in). I like water because it sounds like an instrument you want to play. Water adds a melodic sound to the garden, as if it were music played to relax the gardener. It's a sound you'll never get tired of hearing.

When water droplets fall from an upper tier of the fountain to a lower tier, with the sun catching them just so, they look like diamonds descending. At the spot where my fountain sits, this occurs in the late afternoon sun, particularly in the late winter and early spring when the sun sets directly behind it. When friends visit, I never have to point it out. With the fountain out front, it's visible from the entrance walk. If the sun is setting just right, they can't miss it. The glistening catches their eye every time, even if the fountain is not new to them and they've walked past it a hundred times before.

A water feature for the garden can come in many forms and styles. It could be a wall fountain nestled in a courtyard garden and visible from inside the home, a gurgling urn, or even a formal pool, still and tranquil,

A three-tiered fountain is a show-stopping visual piece that also adds movement and pleasant sound.

reflecting a garden structure or mirroring pots of flowers along the water's edge.

In today's market, manufacturers have responded to our desires. Ready-made "plug and play" fountains exist, most with recirculating pumps so all you need to add is water. Making your own fountain or pond is also easier than you might think, particularly if your goal is an easy design, like a reflecting pond with a shallow depth. The Washington Monument comes to mind, although the scale would be all wrong for your home garden!

The style of your home will direct the style of fountain you choose. There are many fountain types that transcend a particular home style, acting as a neutral design element and adapting to their surroundings once in place. Others are so richly ornate that they will only seem appropriate when paired with a home and garden that can support such a design.

In my home garden, the fountain is quasi-ornate, black metal with three tiers and an in-ground reservoir that I dug myself. I used the excess dirt to berm the surrounding beds, making my fountain area even more imposing—something I've never regretted.

Whether you decorate your fountain with baubles or fish or add a small pond to reflect the sky as you sit alongside it in the evening light, find it in your heart and budget to add a water feature. Water is sensual and seductive. Your pleasure in it never fades. I cannot think of a garden size or style that wouldn't benefit from the sound or look of water. Water deepens the love affair we have with our gardens.

A simple, more rustic stone fountain creates a specific sort of atmosphere.

GARDENING WITH CONFIDENCE

Found and Fulfilling

I found my fountain, put together in three different colors, at a flea market. Originally, it had not been one piece, but the price was right. Once I got home, I discovered the middle section was not true, just a little off kilter, requiring me to make it level. But fountains are very adaptable. With paint and plumber's putty, I was able to create this massive statement fountain for a fraction of the price of a new one. Until you do this kind of thing for yourself (digging the reservoir, making the tiers true, painting the metal), you cannot appreciate how much enjoyment you can get from a design project. For me it was a journey into total relaxation, as if I knew what the reward would be. Each day I'm reminded how good it is to have a fountain.

When we don't run our fountain, the water is more likely to freeze during cold evenings, but keeping the fountain on prevents freezing except on the coldest of days. Even when the fountain isn't running, it serves as a drinking and bathing spot for the wintering birds. On very cold mornings, my son, who is only 10 years old, knows to go out to crack the ice. I never have to tell him; nurturing comes naturally to him. He has a sense of honor in performing such a noble task. After all, he knows it pleases his mom and the wildlife, too.

In my business, I'm called upon most often to add a fountain or a pond to a client's garden. Perhaps it's my passion when I talk of water, or maybe the calling card I have in my front yard does the work for me—but I've been acknowledged as someone who knows her water.

FRAGRANCE IN THE GARDEN

Summer sizzles with scent. With so much competition from plants wanting to be pollinated, flowers must flaunt their blooms like the skirt of a can-can dancer. Flowers have scent for a purpose—to bring in the pollinators. We gardeners are the beneficiaries of their flowery aromas.

But that is not why we love these smells; the reasons are more personal. Certain scents evoke fond memories of working in the garden with your mother or grandmother. Ever notice how the smell of lilacs brings back happy memories, even when it's coming from someone's perfume? Or when a whiff of rosemary reminds you of your dad's chicken? Scents etch memories in our hearts.

Place fragrant flowers where they can provide perfume throughout your day—at the door, down the garden path, downwind of your garden's prevailing wind, and even under windows where the scent can drift into the indoor air. Time your bloom's peak fragrance for when you are around. Plant sweet-scented night-blooming flowers near your bedroom window, to perfume your dreams with their blossoms. Train a vine of moonflower (*Ipomoea alba*) along the arch of the window, plant a fragrant filled window box underneath it, or plant tall clusters of flowering tobacco (*Nicotiana*) to nod into the window.

Devote an entire garden to fragrant flowers. Why not? A fragrant garden can become a place to spend the evening with a glass of wine. The fragrance garden can also serve as

Lavender adds a well-loved scent to a garden.

a cutting garden, allowing you to bring these flowers inside to enjoy.

Most herbs are aromatic rather than fragrant, with scent emanating from the foliage instead of the flowers, but their smells are just as pleasing and desirable. Earthy, musky, and sentimental, herbs evoke many memories. Sunny patches of lavender, rosemary, or mint will release a light perfume that will make you want to linger.

Most suburban gardens have room only for a few large shrubs or small trees, so choose wisely. Set priorities on what you want from your plants—scent, winter interest, provision for the wildlife, or evergreen, for example. If you are planning ahead for larger plants, such as trees and shrubs, this will limit your spontaneous buying to the smaller ones, such as perennials and annuals. The more benefits each plant provides, the higher that choice will rise on your list. If scent is at the top of your list, search for fragrant plants first.

Fragrant flowers can be found on every type of plant in the garden: trees, shrubs, perennials, annuals, ground cover, and vines. Adding plants that will provide a succession of scents in the garden as the seasons progress is an admirable goal. Choose plants that will be fragrant while your herbaceous plants are dormant to extend the season of scent. Winter honeysuckle (*Lonicera fragrantissima*) or wintersweet (*Chimonanthus praecox*) have been wonderful additions to my garden in Raleigh. The soft scent from *Viburnum × bodnantense* 'Dawn' or *Viburnum farreri* will sweeten the air to thrill you during a chilly winter's day.

Each season has a plant for scent. My winter garden is home to Daphne (*Daphne odora*), Edgeworthia, and witch hazel (*Hamamelis vernalis*), as well as a flowering apricot 'Bridal Veil' (*Prunus mume*) taking center stage in the mixed border. Many varieties of mahonia, such

Explore and Take Notes

Somehow summer seems to take care of itself when providing for scent. I don't have to work hard to have sweet-smelling summer plants. This is true for spring, too. Fall can be a bit harder, as is winter. But as a gardener, I step up to the challenge to find great plants for all four seasons. As soon as I recognized the need, finding the plants was easy. I just needed to know where to look. It turns out that they were right under my nose.

Visit your local arboretum in all seasons to see what's in bloom. During each season, plants that grow in your area are on display there. Visiting each season allows you to build a plant list for adding to your garden once your budget meets your desire—or when a week of careful grocery budgeting can free up a few nickels for plant purchases.

I have a notebook I carry with me wherever I go that has a list of plants in the back. Whenever I travel or visit garden centers, I can easily refer to or add plants I like to my wish list. Of course, sometimes I just purchase them on the spot.

Visit arboretums, go on garden tours, frequent garden centers each season—better yet, each month—and see what is available. You may be surprised at what you have been missing.

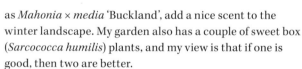

Peonies are popular scent flowers.

as *Mahonia* × *media* 'Buckland', add a nice scent to the winter landscape. My garden also has a couple of sweet box (*Sarcococca humilis*) plants, and my view is that if one is good, then two are better.

Bulbs will brighten your spring garden, and they can add scent, too. Try adding hyacinth and fragrant daffodils, such as *Narcissus poeticus* var. *recurvus* 'Pheasant's Eye'. 'Pheasant's Eye' has bright white petals that contrast brilliantly against a showy yellow eye ringed in red. One of my favorite scented daffodils was given to me by Becky Heath of Brent and Becky's Bulbs in Gloucester, Virginia; this daffodil is called 'Little Gem'. It is a tiny, early bloomer that resides in my rock garden.

Late spring to early summer is peony and lilac season. In the South, we push the limits for growing great peonies; many varieties of peony prefer cooler winters. However, I have had great success with them—not so much with the

lilacs, though. A trip up north is always in order during lilac season.

Of course, roses are in a class by themselves when it comes to adding fragrance in the summer garden. Position your roses where they can be admired and smelled. If the rose has perfume in the name, it's a good indication that the scent is sweet. Again, you have to ask yourself, what do I want from my rose? What is my first priority—scent, disease resistance, or repeat blooming? If scent tops your list, you may have to compromise on disease resistance or repeat blooming.

There is no reason to expect to have everything from every plant. Make your garden a movable feast. When the summer is scented from a certain rose or other flower, enjoy it while it lasts. Then take your chair and move to the next plant that is giving what you need. Enjoy the moments when you are in them. It will make your garden memorable every day.

GARDEN GATES

As I approached the garden gate, partially opened to welcome me in, I noticed how the surrounding plants framed the entrance. There was a little garden with grasses, perennials, and annuals, on either side of the dove-gray gate. Pausing to admire the flowers, I realized the fence abutting the gate was made of shrubs. The shrubs, serving as the fence, were merely there in a supporting role.

Garden gates are an element that can make a major statement about who you are as a gardener. They are so much more than a utilitarian entry points. Gates can be a part of a hardscape fence or an opening through a hedgerow. Fences made from shrubs soften the surroundings. Passing through a garden gate surrounded by plants can make you feel like you're entering a new, special world.

In a way, the garden gate completes the garden. Whether open or closed, it offers an inviting and friendly appearance, leading your eye to the garden beyond. It lets visitors know that they are on the brink of something wonderful. When closed, the gate affords a sense of privacy to those within. An open gate signals a warm welcome to enter.

Even though anyone can peek over the garden gate, a closed garden gate tells a visitor, "Make your presence known before entering." An opened gate is a signal to come on in. In many regions, it means, "I'm in the garden—the door is open; all are welcome." For many years, I lived in one of

A garden gate can create a magical feeling.

GARDENING WITH CONFIDENCE

Make the Old New Again

An old gate can also make a unique and interesting trellis or wall ornament. Most old gates will still have hinges and clasps attached. I find it's best to keep them on, giving interest to the piece and allowing it to again be used as a gate one day. When attaching to a wall, use screws at least 4 inches (10.2cm) long with enough thread to create space for air circulation. There is no question: once you have a cute garden gate attached to the side of your house, there will be a climbing plant in your future. This space between the gate and the wall will provide breathing room for your plant and will also create depth for shadows, creating a most interesting effect.

Climbing roses add brightness to this garden gate.

Raleigh's historic districts, a community called Oakwood. In one particularly lovely garden, it was widely known that, if the garden gate was open, anyone could enter.

Finding the perfect gate for your garden can be a fun adventure. Scouring estate sales, going to a favorite garden center, or rummaging through flea markets and architectural salvage yards makes the hunt part of the fun. Having a gate custom made to reflect your style and personality is also a good option. A garden gate is a small element in the garden that makes a big impact.

A garden gate is the threshold, the beginning of at least two paths, one entering and one leaving. To comfortably move through a garden gate, allow for a minimum width of 3 feet (91.4cm), although extra width is even more welcoming for visitors. You, too, will appreciate a wider entrance on those days when you are pushing a wheelbarrow or garden cart.

Add another layer to your garden entry and enhance the design aesthetic of the garden gate by adding an arbor. Give your arbor a little extra height for when vines spill their flowers from the arch.

When selecting the gate's hardware, consider the overall scale of the piece and the material used. Thin, flimsy metal will be dwarfed by a heavy, solid wooden gate. One piece of hardware that is especially nice for a gate to have is a footing to allow your gate to stay open. Propping your garden gate open welcomes guests and aids you in moving supplies in or debris out. Lift the foot when you need to close it.

One additional feature you may want to consider for your garden gate is an automatic gate closer. The ones in Colonial Williamsburg, Virginia, are the most notable and recognizable. They typically consist of two pieces of chain with a large, heavy ball between them. The ball resembles a cannonball. Its position on the chain allows you to push the gate open, but when you let go of the gate, the ball falls down, closing the gate.

Whatever the materials you choose for your garden gate, it is sure to become a favorite and often-visited part of the garden.

LEVEL CHANGES

Slopes and hills, bumps and dips—a garden often comes in many shapes. Whether your garden is naturally contoured, or you've decided you want to introduce a different profile to your land, level changes are best viewed as opportunities to create instead of challenges to overcome.

How you choose to handle elevation changes can depend on several factors, but primarily on the degree of change you desire. A gradual level change may be fine left alone if walking up and down is manageable. As the gradient increases, you can add steps to ease the journey and add interest. If you have steep inclines, your landscape will benefit greatly from steps that lead to various parts of your garden and make it a more functional space. A steep slope may also benefit from terracing. In any case, these spaces can become your garden's most admirable attributes.

In large areas, you can bring earth-moving machines in to create terraces or retaining walls by cutting slits in the slope and taking out the soil from the bottom to make the upper surfaces level. In smaller areas, this work can be done by hand.

Working with your garden's natural contours is best, and will create a more natural look and lessen your footprint on the landscape. Natural slopes are also good for providing more visibility for your plantings. This is how I chose to design my back garden. To address the level change, I had two choices:

Beautifully crafted elevation changes and elements will feel like they're calling the viewer on to another level.

pushing back the dirt and building a retaining wall and terraces or working with the land as it contoured naturally. I chose the natural slope, and I've never regretted it.

Many materials are available to help with elevation changes, whether you're creating steps or retaining walls. With the greater emphasis today on sustainability, stores are offering more regional materials—like local stone, for example. These materials will blend with your landscape better, improving the aesthetics of the design. Another approach is to link the materials to the house itself. Repeating details found on the house to the terrace or garden steps helps to keep the entire property in harmony. The same brick of the house can be used for retaining walls, or a gray color used in roofing shingles can be repeated in flagstone steps. Pulling a design element from your home will keep harmony in the garden.

When gardening on a slope, such as the area found alongside steps, grow for appeal as well as stability. Diverse plantings are not only more pleasing to the eye, they also add interest, making the journey more fun. Consider your steps an opportunity to add plants ranging from eye-popping tropicals to scented plants, such as rosemary, so with each pass you'll be brushed with a wonderful scent. However, avoid planting any flowering species that will attract bees into your pathways.

Introducing elevation changes in an otherwise flat garden gives the eye different spots where it can pause and enjoy, instead of taking in the whole flat area with one glance. The area also becomes a room without walls. If you are building a sunken garden, or another type of garden that results in elevation changes, you can transfer the removed soil to other areas of the garden, such as beds surrounding the newly created garden or in berms or raised beds.

In any case, the level changes should be part of the journey, not just a way to facilitate movement from one point in the garden to another. Evaluate your needs and the contour of your land to ensure you are gardening your level best.

Stone steps are a classic additional to multilevel gardens.

GARDENING WITH CONFIDENCE

Artificial Elevations with a Natural Look

When a client of mine moved houses, I was sad to leave his old place behind as well, but it was exciting to see what sort of new garden awaited me. Since Raleigh is hilly, I naturally expected to see sloped gardens. The yard at my client's new home did not disappoint.

The home was contemporary with strong Asian influences. The driveway had brick pillars that were 3 feet (91.4cm) tall and had limestone caps. Night-lights were installed on the sides of the pillars, making for an impressive entrance. The earth extended on either side of the pillars in what appeared, at first glance, to be a natural hill transition. I remember thinking, "How convenient that this lot's elevation changes are at the exact place where the entry pillars stand."

After a few weeks tending this garden, I took a closer look. The elevation change was artificial. An elegant berm, measuring only 1½ feet (45.7cm) tall and 4½ feet (1.4m) wide, had been created along the entire front of the property line. Trees and shrubs traversed the berm in the most natural way. It was my lesson in understanding how to make elevation changes where none existed before.

LAYERS OF LIGHT

An evening stroll through the garden in winter is enhanced by the low glow of yellow light. Adding layers of light lends your garden charm and mystery, and it gives you the ability to enjoy the garden at night.

Winter was never my season. For the most part, this was due to the lack of light. After work, when I had the time to be in the garden, the ambient light was not enough to allow me to wander the paths or to admire the trees and shrubs. Memory helped me to navigate the paths so I could empty the trash. But without night-lighting, I stuck to only these utilitarian tasks.

With the installation of night-lighting several years ago, I'm now able to enjoy my garden when the daylight dims, often before dinner. Even the most mundane time outdoors in the evening is enchanting and romantic. As the sun goes down, the garden is transformed into a magical place, completely changed by the light's focus. Light casts against the silhouettes of trees, shrubs, and statuary and serves as a beacon in the distance.

Approach lighting outside as you would interior lighting. Inside your home, stark overhead light can be cold and harsh. More lighting options, such as table lamps, picture lights, and dimmers, will soften a room's glow, making it a welcoming place. The same is true with lighting outdoors. Adding layers of light softens the garden and creates a welcoming glow.

The shadows of leaves can create interesting patterns on the surfaces in your garden.

Good lighting is three-dimensional, giving the garden depth and drama. The focus should not be on the fixtures, but on the effects. Your goal will be to complement nature, not compete with her.

Up-lighting can accent beautifully formed plantings, such as a specimen tree or shrub. Often airy plants, such as a Japanese maple, are good candidates for up-lighting because the glow highlights their interesting forms. Up-lighting also works well for the home itself. Adding spotlights to flood the home's front exterior creates a welcoming appeal.

Down-lighting creates a pool of light to highlight a dining area, a favorite bench, or garden accent. Add down-lighting to the side of a tree will shine down on the lawn providing a pool of light for the children to play during dusk.

Layers of light can add even more value to paths and focal lights. Fire and candlelight, or white twinkle lights, give the garden even more depth. Stringing twinkle lights on arbors, gazebos, sheds, and vines gives a garden more dimension. Grapevine balls, wrapped in lights, can be hung in the trees, or you can loosely wrap a tree trunk and a few branches with lights to highlight a tree that would otherwise be dark in the evening.

Energy-wise solar-powered lights are a snap to install, and they have improved greatly over the years. These can work particularly well as path lighting. I started out with solar lights to see how well I would like night-lighting. I liked them so much that I decided to make the investment in a higher quality, low-voltage permanent solution. In doing so, I turned to a professional local designer to put my garden and home in the best light. The designer, Hoyt Bangs, suggested where to highlight trees, paths, and garden art with various up-lighting, down-lighting, and soft lights to line the paths.

When you are inside looking out, you'll find that night-lighting allows you to extend the view from the kitchen sink, from your favorite chair in the den, or even from the dining room. Dining in candlelight, while looking out into the garden glowing with light, is the epitome of romance.

This winter, when the weather turns frightful, watching snowflakes or rain drops drift through the light beams will allow me to experience some garden time, even if only from the living room chair.

GARDENING WITH CONFIDENCE

Successful Night-Lighting Photography

Of all the efforts I've put into my gardens over the years, night-lighting still ranks the highest in added value. There are no regrets here for investing in night-lighting.

But there are too few gardens with night-lighting. Also, there is too little written about night-lighting, in my opinion. Perhaps it's because the timing in which you can effectively photograph a lit garden is so limited, leaving too few opportunities to spread the word. If people were exposed to night-lighting more, they might be swayed to add it. This is a bit of a "chicken and egg" situation: homeowners might add more night-lighting if they read more about it; magazines might write more about night-lighting if they had more homes to photograph.

On several occasions I've tried to photograph night-lighting scenes, but they always turned out wrong. Then I got the best advice from my friend, Hoyt Bangs, who also designed my night-lighting system—plan to photograph your night-lighting a half hour before sunset.

He was right, of course; I was able to capture good photos as soon as I took his advice. Taking photos just before twilight made them turn out well—the lights showed up especially well with the ambient light appearing darker than it really was.

Warm light makes for a pleasant atmosphere.

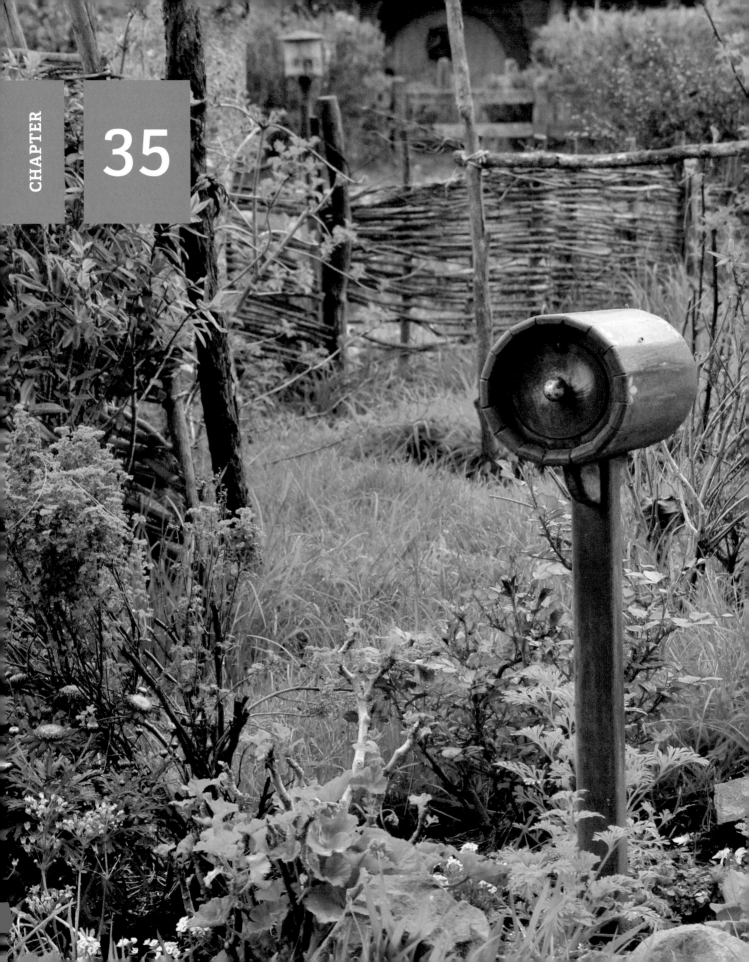

MAILBOX GARDENS

First impressions may be wrong, but they are always right for that moment. Most of us living in suburban neighborhoods pass our mailboxes several times a day. We put in our outgoing mail and take out our incoming mail. Each car that passes sees it; kids hit it with their balls; and you paint it to match your house. So why not plant around it? Your mailbox is most likely the first thing a passerby or visitor will see, so make it the best you can. The mailbox is an American icon and a perfect space for a dedicated garden.

The postal service has rules on the placement of the mailbox (the height and distance from curb), but their main interests are the inside of the box and being able to access it, leaving us gardeners an opportunity to create—one that should not be missed. Mailboxes go a long way toward setting the tone of a property, yet they are often not given much thought. To a degree, you can think of mailboxes as garden art.

My mailbox is so unique—a tall, black, rustic monolith—that visitors often first see it as art before they realize it's just the mailbox. I assume it's because most people who know me already know that I like garden art. Admittedly, it is an interesting mailbox. And the box doesn't stand alone; it's surrounded by a garden. I've always been a gardening opportunist. In my garden, the mailbox has become an attractive focal point with a dedicated garden design.

A small, wooden mailbox in a lush garden takes visitors away to a fantasy world.

Red roses add a pop of color to a mailbox area.

If your mailbox came with the house and cannot be changed for reasons, such as homeowner association rules, consider making it unique with clever plantings. In determining the size of a mailbox garden, match the dimensions of the planting bed to the height of the mailbox. Imagine the mailbox lying down on the ground. The garden bed should stay within the box's reach, more or less, but not be less than three-fourths of the overall height of the mailbox. This will keep the garden bed in good proportion to the mailbox.

The planting design can follow personal tastes, but some basics are good to know. In general, the plants around the box's post should blend into the landscape, balancing the plants with the size of the bed. You don't want to plant something that would overpower the mailbox or obstruct it any anyway.

The area around the base of the post (called the junction) should be softened with low evergreen mounding plantings, such as a dwarf mondo grass (*Ophiopogon japonicus* 'Nana'). If you'd like a little more height, use standard *O. japonicus*. From my perspective, liriope is a bit overdone, so you won't find me suggesting it.

From here, add height and texture by introducing a vertical element to counterbalance the height of the mailbox. A clump

GARDENING WITH CONFIDENCE

Personalities and Plantings

In the movie *The Color Purple*, many scenes and angles are filmed around the mailbox as Celie hopes each day to get a letter from her estranged sister. The box sits on a post made from twisted wood, maybe even a root of some sort. It is distinctive, albeit gnarled, a contrast to a home that is otherwise pleasant to look at. The mailbox suggests there is deeper meaning in the story as you consider why the post and mailbox are so different in style from the house.

Over the years, I've taken hundreds of photos of mailboxes. I have no actual fascination for mailboxes in general, but when I scout gardens for magazines, the first photo I take is the number on the box to remind me of the address. As I went through the scouting photos, I began to pay attention to mailboxes, although I'd never really thought or cared about them before.

After I got to know the gardens and their caregivers, I could begin to match personalities with mailboxes. The most charming gardening personalities all had a twist to their mailbox and the surrounding gardens—antique pedestals, unusual planters, or metal sculptures. These mailboxes had something about them as unique as the gardener— the first impression of good things to come.

of grass, irises, or even a canna would be appropriate as a vertical plant. Then you can layer plantings around the post with different textures and diversity to draw the eye in.

Much too often, gardeners add climbers to their mailbox, overpowering its small size—or worse, attracting stinging insects. We want to stay on the good side of our postal workers, so let's show a little respect. If it seems like adding a vine to the mailbox is obvious, think again. If you do add a vine, look for cultivars that grow no taller than 3 to 4 feet (91.4cm to 1.2m), or be prepared to pinch back with each visit to your mailbox. Even if you are vigilant, vines can get away from you.

A distinctive mailbox will differentiate you from your neighbors, offering an immediate glimpse of your individual taste and style. There are many distinctive mailboxes available to choose from, and you'll enjoy passing by your mailbox and garden each day as they display your personality.

My mailbox goes beyond a box for holding mail. The monolithic shape of my mailbox was already unique enough, but it allowed me also to add a sign that reads, "A water-wise garden watered with harvested rain." It lets me tell you a lot about who I am as a gardener.

CHAPTER 36

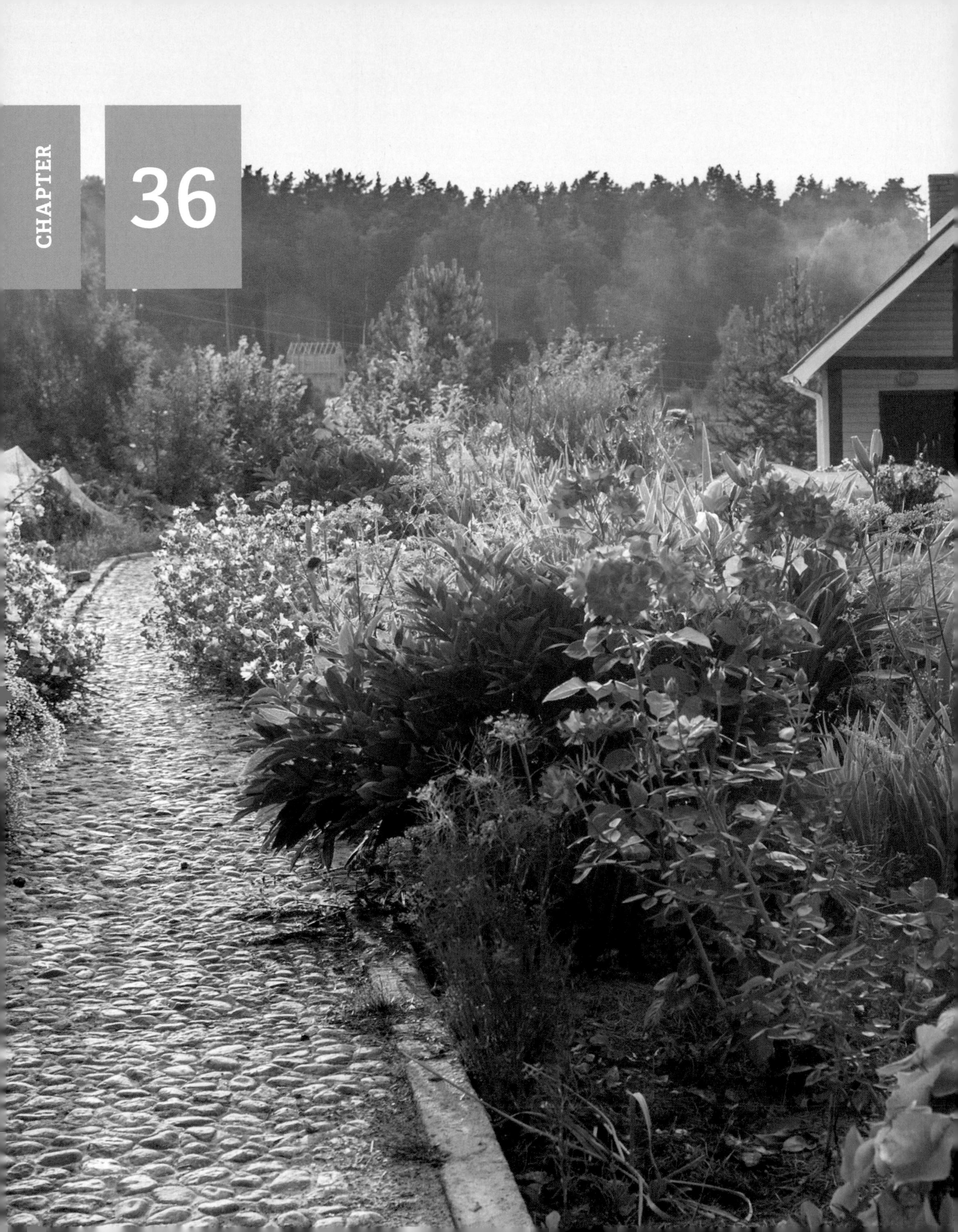

THE GARDEN PATH

A journey down the garden path can be both poetic and practical. More than a means to an end, a path fills a void in the garden, particularly in the winter. Paths give reliable passage and invite you into the garden.

Chances are you already know where to put a path. Over time, a path will make itself. Cut across the lawn enough times to smell the roses, and you will begin to see where a path should go. Casually sketch your house and garden. Map out where a path might lead. Adding curves will slow the pace, add visual interest, and reveal the garden one step at a time.

Know the purpose of the path and how it may be used. Will your path be used by two to journey though the garden together? Or will the path create easy access for you and the wheelbarrow? Thinking about the various uses of the path will help you to plan the details, such as width and materials.

The path width will be best determined by its use. If the passage is to be used only as a service area, to pass from the front yard to the backyard, for example, you only need enough space to allow the passage of a single person. For these types of paths, a width of 2 to 3 feet (61 to 91.4cm) is sufficient. If the path will be for two to travel side by side, you will need a width of 4 to 5 feet (1.2 to 1.5m).

There are several choices when selecting paving material. Gravel paths are ideal for budget-conscious homeowners and provide

A house at the end of a beautiful garden path will always have a certain charm.

149

Lots of color along a garden path will make every step of the walk enjoyable.

traction and allow for good drainage. Gravel looks nice, too, and its crunch is reassuring as you journey down the garden path.

In more informal areas, paths made of mulch, such as woodchips and bark, will define an area. I use a composted leaf mulch in my beds, and line some paths with a mini-nugget bark. Paths made from either mulch or gravel work best in areas not traveled with bare feet or where you will not need to worry about snow removal.

Brick is probably the most versatile material to use in creating garden paths. Complementing most home styles, brick can be laid in many different patterns and can also accept a gentle arch to aid in dispersing water from the path's surface. Set in sand or mortar, brick is equally suitable for a passage to the front door as it is for a service area. Take note, however, that brick paths in moist, heavily shaded areas can retain moisture, creating a slipping hazard.

Concrete pavers offer many options for paths. Pavers offer a great variety of design choices. They are available in non-interlocking styles with smooth edges, interlocking styles with patterned edges that allow the pieces to fit together like a puzzle, and unique shapes for creating more complicated patterns. There are circles, hexagons, squares, and, of course, triangles and rectangles. Pavers can be laid in sand or mortar, making their use versatile. You'll find the many choices available make it easy to find a match for your home's style.

Cut stone tile lends a more formal feeling to a garden path. Flagstone is a natural choice to complement garden plantings. The available colors are naturally subtle, resulting in restful paths. Flagstone can be laid in sand or mortar, but if thick enough, flagstone works well laid directly on top of leveled ground.

Cobblestone, fieldstone, river rock, and other irregularly shaped stones give a more relaxed look to the garden path.

The use of various sizes in the design allows for some very creative patternmaking.

Wood can be used as raised decking in the garden, or as an edging to other path materials. Boards can be positioned widthwise to visually slow movement or lengthwise to provide a sense of forward movement. An even path can be constructed with wood to level out the dips and valleys in irregular surfaces. Left natural, stained, or painted, wood lends itself to just about any home style.

Adding a path visually directs your journey through the garden as well as making the walk easier. It also gives you a chance to add an aesthetic element to your garden through your choice of size, shape, and materials.

Paths make the journey through the garden delightful, and when planned with the journey in mind, they make each step along the way worthwhile.

Let Paths Develop Naturally

Adding paths can be a funny thing. The best ones are put where they are actually needed, not necessarily where you want them. People will make your paths. One thing to consider is this: do you really need a path made from another material, or can it be just as effective if you used nothing at all?

In my back garden, where I cut through the rock garden area to get to the shed, I added stepping stones as a path. It made sense at the time. I also added stepping stones at the bottom of the rock garden because it created a path coming into my back garden from the side. Then I added another stepping-stone path to enter into the upper lawn.

Viewed from space, my garden looked like a road map. I had gone a bit overboard. It looked busy and cluttered. To fix the problem, I removed almost all the stepping stones and let the mulch-covered ground serve as the paths. I kept a few stepping stones at the intersections of paths to suggest direction; this let the eye tell the visitor where to go next. My garden became more peaceful and less cluttered.

RETAINING WALLS

Raleigh, where I live, is naturally hilly, situated in the foothills of the Piedmont region of North Carolina. It is not uncommon to see homes on either side of a street appear to slope away from each other, be it a gentle slope or not so gentle. Because of this, retaining walls are also a familiar and often necessary sight. In spite of being commonplace, or perhaps because of it, retaining walls have become so desirable that we add them even when there is only the slightest incline.

The primary purpose of a retaining wall is to hold back land and at the same time make the area level for planting. Any home with a sloping or uneven yard can benefit from the addition of a retaining wall. When you add a wall, you are also adding another layer of visual interest to your garden, increasing your garden's overall aesthetic appeal. Sloped terrain adds character and interest to the landscape. A retaining wall doesn't take away from this natural characteristic; instead, it gives rise to an opportunity to lift your garden's melody up an octave.

A retaining wall must manage the downhill force of water and soil. In practical terms, 1 cubic foot (30.5cm^3) of soil can weigh nearly 100 pounds (45.4kg). The taller the retaining wall you desire, the less likely it is that building it will be a successful do-it-yourself project. This is not meant to discourage you but rather to help you understand that a tall retaining wall requires some engineering work for proper support and drainage.

A stone garden wall creates a nice contrast against the brilliant colors of the garden.

However, adding a short dry-stacked wall as an accent cut into your sloped lot is a very feasible DIY project. Such a wall could be just a garden accent, or it could be an important design element your garden needs.

Retaining walls can be made from many types of materials, including timber, brick, stone (whether used flat or cobbled), and even cinder block. As with most elements discussed in this book, the materials used for retaining walls are best matched with the style of the home. A brick home is often best served by a wall made from the same or a closely matching brick. A stone wall made with the same stone used to face the home is a natural fit.

My personal preference is to use regional materials. However, concrete block systems enhanced with color and face texture to mimic natural stone are now commonly available and popular. These concrete block systems are becoming ubiquitous. They give a wall a manufactured look, lessening your garden and home's uniqueness. But I am often reminded that these walls are relatively inexpensive.

Stone walls charm me. They give a feeling of permanence. As with so many elements in garden architecture, the materials were often those that were available. For example, in the Northeast, stone is used so often because it is available locally.

A dry-stack wall is the simplest retaining wall to make. The stone can be stacked with no mortar up to about 2 feet (61cm). Above this height, mortaring the walls is recommended. One of my favorite ways to use this type of wall is at the corner of a property

What other brilliant blooms could
be over the garden wall?

GARDENING WITH CONFIDENCE

Create Cohesiveness

Large bits of broken concrete can make a wonderful material for retaining walls. Given its weight, concrete can often be laid without mortar and the crevices filled with soil to support plantings. Broken concrete creates an interesting look, while at the same time being environmentally conscious.

One of my favorite gardens is in Cary, North Carolina—the garden of Walt and Kathleen Thompson. They used broken concrete throughout their garden for paths, edging, and short retaining walls. When I first visited, I didn't even realize that was what it was. Beds were raised with this edge, some very low and others taller. Broken concrete was also cut into the dirt and laid as paths that at first glance looked like stone. An added bonus is that all the concrete is recycled.

Often the best garden design is not one with elements that jump out at you. Instead, it is a design that blends all the elements in an attractive way with the surroundings. Then as you spend time in the garden, you can begin to focus on single elements—the containers, the retaining walls, the edging, and the fencing. If it all blends, then nothing will stand out, making you wonder why it is part of the garden.

This is something to strive for, cohesiveness in design. Select materials for a wall that will blend nicely, forming an attractive backdrop for plants and everything else you add to your garden. In a shade garden, ferns and moss growing between stone gives a comforting, aged look. On a retaining wall with a sunny face, sedums can give the effect of a mature garden wall. Carrying over the style of your home—brick to brick, stone to stone—or using a material that will complement the home, such as clapboard and stone, mellows the wall, making it a seamless addition.

that slopes. For homes set on a level lot that slopes away on one edge, adding a dry-stacked wall visually and actually levels the lot and extends the foundation planting beds, which adds interest.

It seems that dry-stack walls have come under fire from some designers recently as not representing nature in a natural way. The argument is that thin layers of flat stone are not readily found in nature. My rose garden has one—a short wall cut into the ground to create a level bed for the garden. Despite the criticisms of this sort of wall, I still like mine, and it functions beautifully in my garden.

If your land slopes, adding a retaining wall made from complementary materials will both level the land and give visual interest to a new planting area.

GARDEN HOUSE

Long ago, I decided to have a garden house, a structure for the garden that would "house" me in all manner of ways—a well-designed shed, by any other name. I desired a refuge from the everyday, a place to escape and dream about the garden as it is, how it was, and the way it could one day be. I wanted something beyond the function of a shed, where tools lay spurned and in need of cleaning or straightening after having been hastily discarded at the end of an exhausting yet invigorating day of work in the garden.

During my days living in London, I saw garden houses as follies. I fell in love with the need for a folly, a garden house to rest this lifelong gardener's soul. At long last, I finally got one in 2011, a structure made from rusting metal with inserts to seat glass or plastic panes for windows and a roof. The view from the inside looking out through the window slats frames the garden with country charm.

My use of the space changes each season and is different for each of my children's needs. Yes, I share the garden house, but the rule is that privacy must prevail. The garden house is well understood as the place to be utterly alone. In no way can there even be a knock on the door. In the event of an emergency, a loud guttural scream is recommended.

I often think of our garden house as the gardener's equivalent to a sweat lodge. The etiquette in a sweat lodge is to respect the traditions of the lodge leader. So, if I invite someone in, or if I am invited in, the person who

A garden house can become your secret escape.

Open windows make great ventilation
for you and your plants.

was there first is the person in charge and the one setting the rules.

More often than not, I enter the garden house to reflect, and I want silence. But I'll also invite a friend for refreshments, and during those times, conversation is encouraged. This peaceful place is about pondering feelings and sharing them, if desired.

My children have their own preferred ways of enjoying the garden house. One daughter likes to talk on the phone while she's in the garden house. I respect this. My other daughter likes just to sit with me, not needing to use the space on her own yet, but she is old enough to understand the importance of this space to me and her older sister. My youngest child has no interest in using the space or disturbing me in it. His main concern is making sure all

his kicked balls go into the goal and not into the side of the garden house.

Have you considered creating such a space for yourself—a place to read with your afternoon tea or morning coffee, to plan your garden beds, or to store your gardening books? Perhaps you desire a space to plan Christmas decorations or to write creatively. Being able to remove oneself from the status quo helps spur creativity. It may be just the kind of place you need. The view from inside my garden house holds the most interesting perspective. If I could paint, this view would be my inspiration.

There is no reason to have a solely utilitarian space. Add duality to your shed; make it work for both you and your tools. Then, add what makes your heart sing, creating a space that is in tune with your deepest desires.

GARDENING WITH CONFIDENCE

Set a Goal and Enjoy the Journey

When I lived in England, personal garden space was de rigueur—often in the form of a tricked-out shed, proper greenhouse, or even a garden conservatory, which is what my sweet townhome had. It wasn't anything more than a room with an outside wall that was filled with glass instead of solid material. The room faced east, so it was where I headed to catch the morning warm-up.

There I would dream of one day having my own little place. I wanted a spot to go for afternoon tea, a habit I picked up while living in London that is still with me today. (It's so civilized—taken in the late afternoon during the proverbial calm before the storm of fixing dinner, helping with homework, and getting kids off to the bath and the bed.)

My dream garden house would be a detached room. I've always liked the idea of living on a compound with multiple outbuildings, one of which could be my garden house.

I would surround myself with plants, where I could hide and savor the quiet. Benches would hold plants— old benches, rather than new, with worn wood weathered from use. The floor would be pea gravel so I could enjoy the crunch of each movement with my feet.

The garden house would need lighting, not so much for me to see by but enough for me to admire from afar. Soft light would spill into the evening garden, beckoning me to come out for a sit and listen as the evening chorus of garden life reached a crescendo. This light would not be a harsh faux-aluminum half-circle housing a naked bulb. There would be a circle of light at the end of a chandelier arm. It would have rustic charm, and its age would be respected and admired.

I'm almost there, making my own dream garden house. This is not a process that needs to be rushed, but rather savored and perfected for my future use . . . until I have it just right.

TRELLISES

A 'Don Juan' rose hangs from the side of an antique French window guard, with just enough vine to complement the beauty of the antique piece. The window guard is used as a piece of garden art on the side of the house; the rose is an accent to the art.

Vertical gardening is hot right now; however, anyone who has ever grown a vine is already hip to the knowledge that vines are a great way to bring a garden to new heights. But did you ever think of the trellis your vine climbs as doing the same? Trellises can be more than functional pieces to support vines and climbers, more than vertical and horizontal lines coming together to form a structure. They can be as much a part of the design as the climber itself.

Any support can be used as a trellis as long as it continues to perform its primary functions—giving plant support, particularly to a mature plant; providing good air circulation; and standing up against the elements. Trellises can be humble or bold, small or large, complementary or contrasting. The key is that they serve to support and let the garden design speak. The trellis, like all elements introduced into the garden, should continue your theme. Rustic begets rustic. Formal begets formal. Contemporary begets contemporary. (At least if you want a cohesive design.)

Choose a trellis that will support the plant you want to grow. The scale of the trellis

Runner bean plants climbing up a trellis.

should suit the location and the plant. A thin, low trellis support will be gobbled up trying to hold up a 'Lady Banks' rose. This type of trellis is best suited for petite vines—many varieties of clematis, for example. Some vines are massive and will fully cover their support. For example, a climber such as a Carolina jessamine, which can be full, lush, and evergreen, will need something sturdy. Once this plant matures, the trellis may never be seen again. In these cases, a strong, utilitarian support is all that is required.

Other plantings, such as a tamed rose like 'Don Juan', should work in concert with the trellis. While substantial support is needed for most roses, roses are best pruned to have good air circulation and an airy, open effect. The rose is not an evergreen, and more importantly, you need to prune it during the dormant seasons. So, the trellis goes from a supporting role during the rose's growth and bloom phase to a starring role when the rose goes dormant. When the trellis will be seen, why not choose a beautiful trellis that will do more than support?

Trellises can also be used to hang planters.

GARDENING WITH CONFIDENCE

Structure Adds Style

Adding a trellis to your garden is another great opportunity to bring in your own style and personality. A lover of natural decor may delight in a trellis made from grapevine or cedar limbs. Formal fanciers may find an old wrought iron fence section to be the perfect garden addition. A cottage gardener may be charmed into making a trellis from an old shovel or hoe collection. You might even find yourself wanting to leave your trellis bare, at least for part of the year, if it shows off a little bit of who you are.

For my home garden, I use decorative trellises in the vegetable garden to support tomatoes during the summer but solicit their service as nice garden accents during the off season: two willow obelisks set as sentries watching over the vegetable garden. They speak "country"—enhancing my garden's personality.

Look for unusual places in your garden to add a trellis. A large expanse of wall, whether on the house or garage, becomes an excellent focal point—just remember that putting a vine or climber up against a wall may mean a little extra work when it's time for maintenance jobs, such as repainting siding. The trellis can be a property divider where space is limited and the benefit of a breeze welcomed. You can also place a trellis on the shed roof, giving a vine a foothold to cover it with charm.

In areas that will support a focal point, such as a courtyard, think about the trellis first, not the plant.

The architectural features of the trellis should speak to you foremost. The plantings chosen should be ones that complement the trellis, not the other way around. While trellises are usually thought of in terms of function, they can also be very nice ornamental pieces. Of course, if you have need for a massive support, then look beyond attractiveness to consider function, as well.

A trellis can create visual interest in the garden, as well as merely supporting plants. Use your imagination—the trellis is a great way to get your garden off the ground and up where it can be seen.

CHAPTER 40

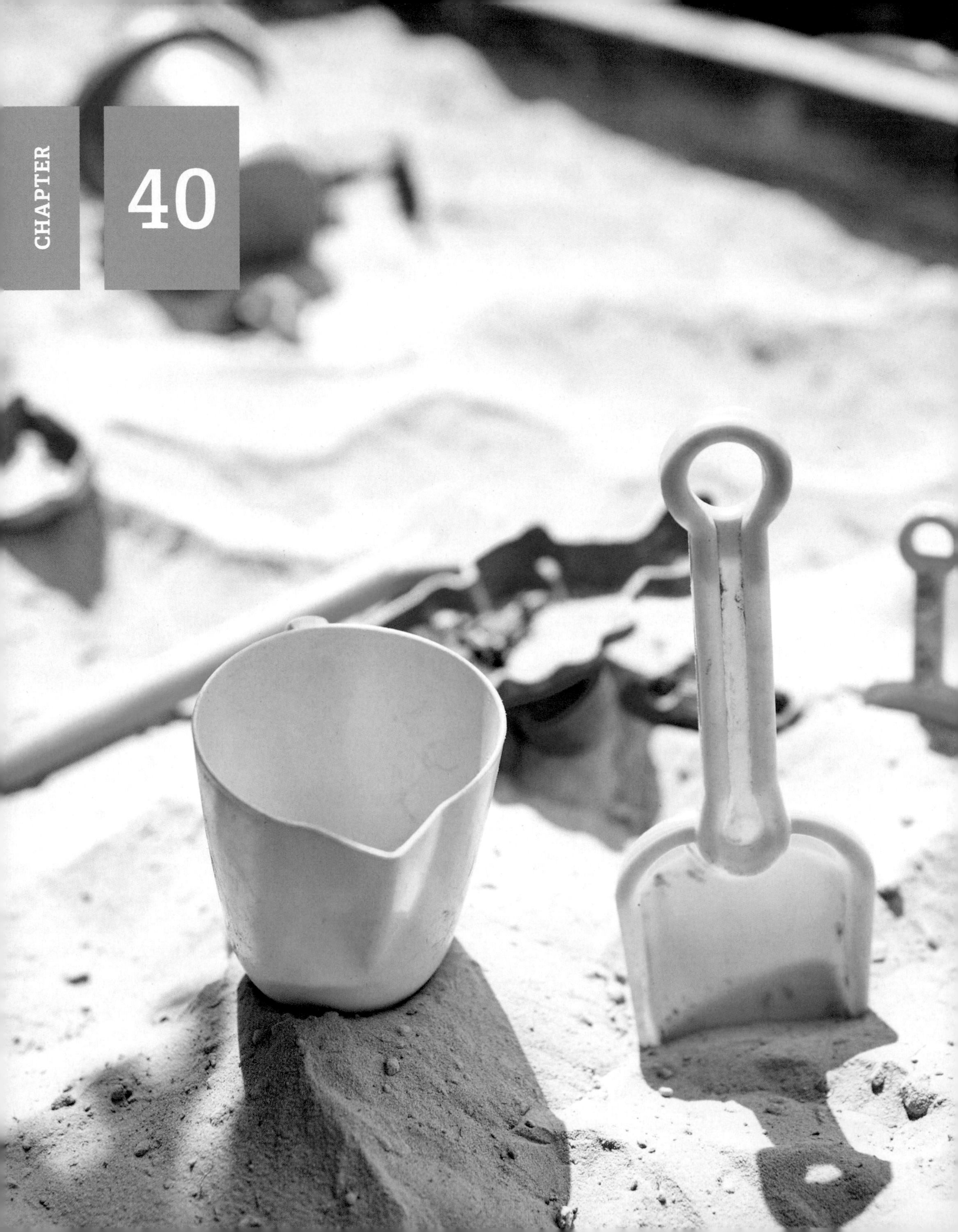

KIDS IN THE GARDEN

My garden at home was designed specifically with kids in mind. We moved in when my oldest was one—and now my youngest is eleven. So, you can imagine that I would have been remiss if I hadn't created the opportunity to make my garden a welcoming place for the kids.

When I was designing my garden, what I actually envisioned was a haven for my whole family to enjoy, especially my kids. I wanted to create a space where they could spend a bit of every day outdoors. While, admittedly, I find it tiresome picking up the bats, balls, and other toys strewn across the lawn and hidden under the bushes, the fact they are there is a clear sign that my kids are indeed using the garden, just as I had hoped and designed for.

If you are outside, it won't take much persuading to get your kids outside, too. Our family looks for reasons to be outdoors. If nothing else, it's where we spread a blanket on the green grass of the backyard soccer field to read, watch the clouds, or do homework. Each experience outside is unique and different. I can only imagine if we just visited the garden for work, only venturing out to mow the lawn or pull the weeds—then "outside" might become a frightful word.

With a little forethought, kids can be made to feel special in the garden, whether or not they have a big, dedicated playset. Give the kids areas to sow their own seeds. Lettuce, radishes, cucumbers, carrots, and beans are all easy for kids to grow. Annuals, such as impatiens or marigolds, keep kids wanting to visit "their" garden each day.

Adding something like a sandbox encourages active play in the garden.

Include plants in your garden that engage your children on a sensory level. Kids will revel in the sight of red strawberries, the feel of soft lamb's ear (*Stachys byzantina*), the sound that pigsqueak (*Bergenia cordifolia*) makes when they rub the leaf between their thumb and forefinger, the smell from rosemary or lavender, or the taste of sugar at the end of a honeysuckle blossom. By making the garden a place of discovery, it will become the place your children want to be.

Get children their very own child-sized garden tools. If they sense that you trust them in the garden, it gives them the confidence to grow. They can learn about preparing the soil, placing the seeds, and how to nurture their plants in the absence of rain. When it's time to harvest, kids will often eat food they'd otherwise turn up their little noses toward if they had a hand in growing it. During the meal, give special praise to the kids for their care of the fruits and vegetables. My dad would always beam when we ate produce from the garden, saying, "It's fresh . . . it's from the garden." This proclamation made me feel proud about having been a part of bringing that produce to the table.

I often work with clients who took years off from the garden when their children were young because they felt overwhelmed by the prospect of maintaining a garden with little ones underfoot. There is no reason to neglect your garden because of your children. Engaging your children in the garden can have a calming effect on you and your kids. Do not worry that the kids will destroy it with their playing. Plants are resilient. Kids also learn where to step and where not to step. Adding paths through the garden will serve as a road map to guide children through, particularly when they have friends over. The happiness you will get from seeing your kids exploring, learning, and having fun in the garden will far outweigh your worries about maintenance.

Here are some ideas for building a child-friendly garden:

- **Have children participate in the process of selecting and growing plants**. This will give them a chance to learn and get excited about gardening.
- **Don't forget wildlife.** Include plants and water to attract birds, butterflies, and beneficial insects that children will enjoy watching.
- **Give kids some active space in the garden**—a tree house or fort they can climb, winding paths to run, or a veggie patch they can tend.
- **Create space just for kids**—such as a child-sized bench for reading or a teepee made by staking beanpoles and planting flowering vines on them.

Remember that adding structures and other creative elements to a garden makes it inviting to both kids and adults. But the best reason of all to garden while your kids are still at home is to get them outside to discover, enjoy, and learn. Don't pass up this wonderful experience.

A rope swing is a classic garden addition for kids to play on.

GARDENING WITH CONFIDENCE

Share Your Delight for the Outdoor World

It was my father who got me out in the garden. Each spring, we would till a section in the back for tomatoes, peppers, and radishes. My dad liked radishes. We would also try our hand at watermelon and corn. But what that garden really did for me was get me outside. Because he was there, I wanted to be there, too. If you want your kids to experience the outdoors, lead by example and go play outside.

My nostalgia for time spent in the garden with my dad led me to create garden space for my own children that would not only encourage them to get outdoors but would also give us the chance to make some great memories together. In our sloped front yard, I built beds at the sides and left a large expanse of grass for the kids to play on. They use the lawn for sledding during those lucky winters when we get snow or, in summer, for rolling down the cool, green grass.

In the backyard, off the porch, there is a steep incline that makes up my mixed border. Above it is the area I refer to as the upper garden, and here I left a large open area of grass, with straight edges lining my beds. This swath of grass is referred to as the "soccer field." It's an open area about 60 feet (18.3m) long and 25 feet (7.6m) wide. My kids, my son in particular, will set up goals at each end and kick the ball from one end to the other, making goals and raising his hands to an imaginary cheering crowd.

Because I was often in the garden, my kids naturally hung out where mom was. Once, when my oldest daughter was three, my husband asked her, "Where's Mom?" She answered, "Just follow the hose." (That tactic is no longer effective since I am now committed entirely to waterwise design— see chapter 48, beginning on page 196.) So, when my children weren't with me, they knew exactly where to find me.

It wasn't difficult to get my kids interested in the garden. My kids don't think the work that needs to be done outside is a chore, probably because I don't either. To them, it's a place where I don't chide them for being too loud or messy. It's a place they can run and play freely. Their playset, the site of many fun family memories, has morphed over the years to accommodate their changing interests. It went from a wee tot's climbing wall and fort, with sandbox, red horse swing, and curvy, yellow slide, to chin-up bars and swings reaching so high I had to avert my eyes. As my kids have "aged out" of the playset, it has morphed again, transitioning from an all-consuming place to a site rarely visited. I plan to convert this space to housing for chickens soon and hopefully bring my kids back to this once-loved space to create more memories in the garden.

ATTRACTING BIRDS, BEES, AND BUTTERFLIES

You know it's spring when the birds begin to sing, the butterflies gracefully flit around your garden, and the bees buzz from one flower to the next. But did you know you can take steps to enhance your garden's attractiveness to the birds, bees, and butterflies? Even better, you can create a garden that entices them to call your yard home.

As daylight extends and warm temperatures arrive, the bees and butterflies are close behind. The chapter on creating a wildlife habitat (see page 73) provided you some basic information on what wild creatures need to feel at home in your garden. But there is more to it than just meeting the bare minimum when you want to attract lots of birds, bees, and butterflies. In this chapter, you will see that by adding specific plant types, you can increase your bird, bee, and butterfly populations.

One of the greatest lessons I learned for creating a bird, bee, and butterfly habitat came from the National Wildlife Federation's web site, *nwf.org*. They suggest that when you are planting a hedge you should plant to benefit the widest range of wildlife. The hedge should ideally include at least one evergreen, two nectar-producing plants, two berry-producing plants, and one thorny species. This combination will provide nesting areas, protection from predators, and food, nectar, and pollen sources.

Evergreens, primarily conifers, are important for birds in particular. They provide

Bumblebees do a lot of work in the garden.

Monarch butterfly caterpillars can eat only milkweed leaves, but the adults can enjoy the nectar from many types of flowers.

dense shelter, good nesting locations, and food. There are varieties suitable for every space and growing condition.

Nectar-producing plants come in many types, and you can create beautiful layers of these plants in your yard. You'll find that the category of "nectar-producing plants" includes deciduous trees and shrubs (those that lose their leaves in autumn), as well as vines, annuals, and perennials, such as red maple (*Acer rubrum*), lowbush blueberry (*Vaccinium angustifolium*), crossvine (*Bignonia capreolata*), and evergreen candytuft (*Iberis sempervirens*).

Berry-producing plants are ideal for attracting and feeding birds, with many also providing spring flowers with nectar and pollen for bees and butterflies. Birds will nest in the crotches of trees and shrubs. Gray catbirds, American robins, northern cardinals, cedar waxwings, and northern mockingbirds all like to use American highbush cranberry (*Viburnum trilobum*), elderberry (*Sambucus canadensis*), and American mountain ash (*Sorbus americana*) as sources of food and shelter, and as places to raise their young.

During the summer the birds can sustain themselves on fruits such as cherry (*Prunus avium*), raspberry (*Rubus* spp.), blueberry, serviceberry (*Amelanchier arborea*), grape (*Vitis* spp.), plum (*Prunus* spp.), and fig (*Ficus carica*).

GARDENING WITH CONFIDENCE

My Top Ten

Here are ten of my favorite plants to add to bird, butterfly, and bee gardens. They can grow in a wide range of conditions, nationwide:

- **Phlox (Zones 3–9):** Phlox comprises a large, diverse group of flowers that bloom from early spring through fall. *Phlox subulata* is among the earliest spring blooms, welcoming the season's first hummingbirds and butterflies.
- **Liatris (Zones 3–10):** Also known as blazing star and gayfeather, liatris can grow from 2 to 5 feet (61cm to 1.5m), depending on the variety. The nectar-rich flowers attract sulphurs, whites, swallowtails, painted ladies, monarchs, and other butterflies. The seeds ripen in the fall and are loved by seed-eating birds, including finches, chickadees, titmice, nuthatches, and buntings.
- **Butterfly weed or *Asclepias* spp. (Zones 3–9):** This starts attracting hummingbirds and butterflies in midsummer and is a favorite nectar plant for adult butterflies. It is also a host plant for larvae of the so-called "milkweed butterflies"—monarch, queen, and soldier.
- **Black-eyed Susan, or *Rudbeckia* spp. (Zones 3–9):** These bright yellow perennials love full sun to part shade and bloom summer through fall. In fall and winter, the seed heads attract chickadees, goldfinches, and house finches.
- **Coneflower, or *Echinacea* spp., (Zones 3–10):** Bees, birds, and butterflies love this perennial. Cut it back in early summer to prolong the bloom time.
- **Aster (Zones 3–8):** Asters provide brilliant explosions of color at the end of the season, and foraging butterflies can't resist it.
- **Mahonia (Zones 5–11):** Mahonia needs full sun to part shade. This evergreen shrub with toothed leaf edges and blue berries provides food for wildlife in late summer and fall.
- **Joe-Pye weed, or *Eupatorium purpureum* (Zones 4–9):** This plant is a classic seed provider. Pinch it back early in the season to make shorter plants and boost flowering and seed production.
- **Sedum (Zones 3–10):** Sedum takes the starring role when other plants are fading. It is very cold-hardy, and finches and chickadees like the seeds. Don't cut off the seed heads until spring so that you can enjoy your wild visitors throughout the winter.
- **Holly, or *Ilex* spp. (Zones 5–9):** This evergreen is a must-have winter classic with nourishing red berries. Species characteristics range from small bushes to 60-foot-tall (18.3m-tall) trees. Winterberry, or *Ilex verticillata* (Zones 3–10), for example, drops leaves in the fall to show off its brilliant berries; it is a favorite of blue jays.

Remember that these trees and plants will flower before they fruit, providing pollen and nectar to a wide variety of bees, butterflies, and other insects. And don't forget that hummingbirds will search out any trumpet-shaped, nectar-laden plants as well, such as bee balm (*Monarda* spp.), cardinal flower (*Lobelia cardinalis*), trumpet creeper (*Campsis radicans*), and lupines (*Lupinus polyphyllus*).

The NWF also mentions adding a thorny shrub to the hedgerow mix to provide a haven for birds. I like to add holly when I'm designing a mixed hedgerow. The prickly leaves will keep critters, such as cats, from easily following birds into the hedge, giving them a bit of protection.

Why not add some perennials and annuals in and around your hedgerow? Perennials provide nectar and seed sources for many backyard birds, bees, and butterflies. Purple coneflowers and black-eyed Susans can live in a wide range of growing conditions and will provide nectar and seeds.

Since you are building a garden anyway, why not add beauty and life to your garden by purposefully selecting plants that attract birds, bees, and butterflies? This way you get the pretty plants and the helpful, necessary wildlife they attract.

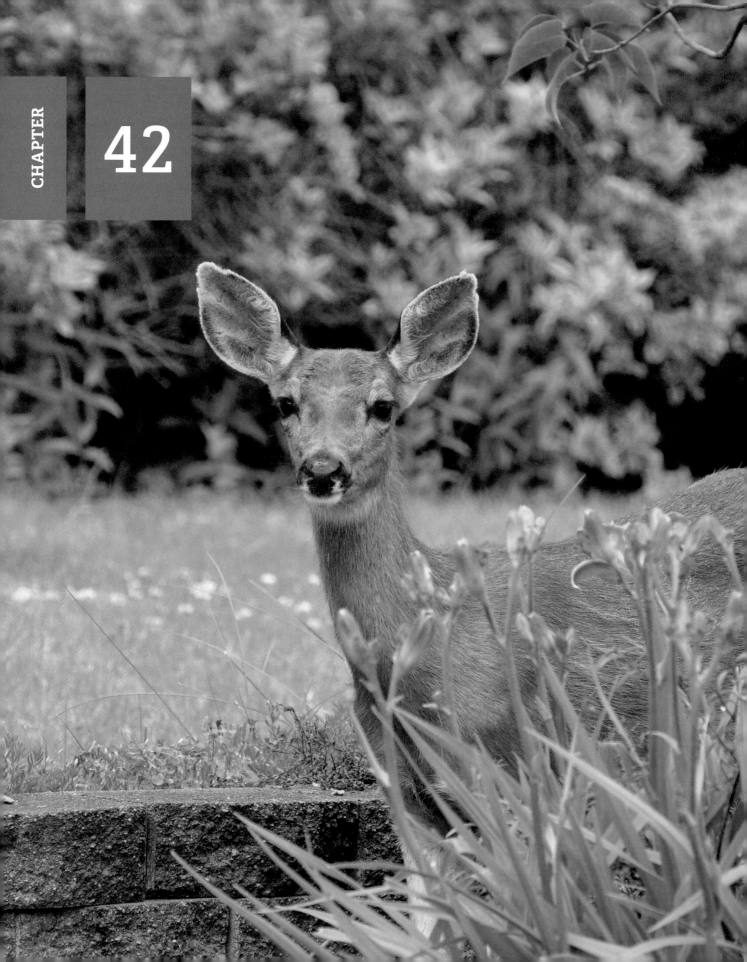

CRITTER CONTROL

I spend a good bit of time talking about attracting wild visitors and appreciating the wildlife my garden draws in. But there is also a real problem with unwelcome wildlife in the garden. For many of us, that means deer and rabbits. Certainly, there are many other pests that bother the residential gardener, such as moles, voles, squirrels, opossums, and raccoons, but deer and rabbits are some of the most common garden-wreckers in many regions.

Deer are becoming a problem even in suburbia; perhaps that is better phrased as "especially in suburbia." Most of our suburban gardens were not planned to deal with deer. However, as developments continue to take away animal habitats, deer look for food wherever they can—often in our own backyards.

Sprays are somewhat effective in defending against deer, but you have to reapply them monthly and on any new growth. The best defense against deer is a good offense. Don't plant the things deer love most—a list that unfortunately includes garden favorites like roses and hostas. At first, you may think you are constricting your plant choices, and perhaps you are to a degree. But you are also giving yourself the opportunity to learn about and use plants you might not have otherwise considered.

The following is a list of plants deer will be less likely to eat. It would be remiss to say, "They will never eat these," because if deer are hungry enough, they'll eat anything. In general, though, if the plant has a rough texture or a bad taste, deer will avoid it.

A deer visitor in the garden may not always be welcome.

GARDENING WITH CONFIDENCE

Nature Always Surprises

I remember a wonderful spring day when my friend Patrick was touring my garden. We came upon my Snow Fountains® weeping cherry tree. Each branch that brushed near the ground was nibbled off. At first Patrick suggested it was the rabbits, but it was too high off the ground, at about 2 feet (61cm). I jokingly said, "If I didn't know better, I would say it was the deer." We both laughed, because there were never any deer in my neighborhood, or at least there hadn't been since the houses were built.

A couple of days later, I was working on a story at my desk, and my son came running in, yelling, "Mom, come quick! There is a deer in the back garden." This was such a foreign sight to me that it might as well have been a kangaroo. Sure enough, there stood a deer eating the cherry tree. The next day we found a fawn sleeping under it! While I don't necessarily want my garden to become a deer feeding ground, it's not often we have the opportunity to watch deer up close, and we considered ourselves fortunate to enjoy their presence.

Cottontail rabbits are very cute but can be very destructive in a garden.

- **Perennial flowers:** allium, anemone, astilbe, baptisia, bee balm (*Monarda* spp.), bellflower (*Campanula* spp.), bleeding heart (*Dicentra spectabilis*), butterfly weed (*Asclepias tuberosa*), coreopsis, candytuft (*Iberis umbellata*), daffodil (*Narcissus*), feverfew (*Tanacetum parthenium*), flax (*Linum usitatissimum*), geum, goldenrod (*Solidago* spp.), lamb's ear (*Stachys byzantina*), liatris, mint (*Mentha* spp.), tansy (*Tanacetum vulgare*), tiger lily (*Lilium lancifolium*), evening primrose (*Onagraceae*), oregano (*Oregano vulgare*), Oriental poppy (*Papaver orientale*), ostrich fern (*Matteuccia struthiopteris*), pinks (*Dianthus caryophyllus*), Pulmonaria, rhubarb (*Rheum rhabarbarum*), sage (*Salvia officinalis*), Shasta daisy (*Leucanthemum × superbum*), soapwort (*Saponaria officinalis*), scilla, sweet William (*Dianthus barbatus*), wormwood (*Artemisia absinthium*), veronica , vinca (*Catharanthus roseus*), yarrow (*Achillea millefolium*), and yucca.
- **Trees and shrubs:** American bittersweet (*Celastrus scandens*), Austrian pine (*Pinus nigra*), barberry (*Berberis*), Colorado blue spruce (*Picea pungens*), English hawthorn (*Crataegus laevigata*), European white birch (*Betula pendula*), European beech (*Fagus sylvatica*), forsythias, honey locust (*Gleditsia triacanthos*), beauty bush (*Kolkwitzia amabilis*), mugo pine (*Pinus mugo*), Norway spruce (*Picea abies*), white spruce (*Picea glauca*), red pine (*Pinus resinosa*), red osier dogwood (*Cornus sericea*), paper birch (*Betula papyrifera*), Russian olive (*Elaeagnus angustifolia*), Scotch pine (*Pinus sylvestris*), lilac (*Syringa vulgaris*), rosemary (*Rosmarinus officinalis*), and lavender (*Lavandula angustifolia*).
- **Annual flowers:** ageratum, basil (*Ocimum basilicum*), begonia, blue salvia (*Salvia guaranitica*), dusty miller (*Centaurea cineraria*), dahlia, four o'clock (*Mirabilis multiflora*), forget-me-not (*Myosotis scorpioides*), foxglove (*Digitalis purpurea*), geranium (*Pelargonium × hortorum*), heliotrope (*Heliotropium arborescens*), marigold (*Calendula officinalis*), morning glory (*Ipomoea leptophylla*), parsley (*Petroselinum*), Lobelia, poppy (*Eschscholzia californica*) , snapdragon (*Antirrhinum majus*), and verbena.

Most county extension offices (see *https://www.nifa.usda.gov/about-nifa/ how-we-work/extension/cooperative-extension-system*) have a list of regional plants that are generally less popular with visiting deer. No one can claim a plant is totally resistant to deer. Sometimes deer will take one big bite only to walk away, but often by then the damage has already been done. The lists are a good place to start, though.

For deterring rabbits, many of the same plants that deer don't enjoy are not loved by bunnies either, but this is not always the case. A good example is *Phlox subulata*, also known as creeping phlox. Deer will avoid it, but bunnies love it, devouring a single plant in an hour. I'm crazy about this butterfly magnet, so I always try again. Phlox is the one plant that prompts me to begin a regimen of spraying each year, but usually I forget to keep it up after a while—and then I come out again to find it eaten down to a nub.

Last year, a long-haired yellow cat with yellow eyes adopted us. We named him Sunny. What the plants couldn't deter, Sunny sure could. The bunnies have stayed at a safe distance from the garden ever since, even with Sunny moving to an indoor life. Remember, cats can be a detriment to the wildlife we want in our yards, so it's best to keep them inside.

ENERGY CONSERVATION

When building your garden, look for the beauty beyond the buds. Proper landscaping can help you conserve energy. A well-placed tree, shrub, or vine can cool the heat from the sun in the summer and lessen heat loss in the winter.

It used to be that homes were built with temperature control in mind. Before air conditioning, interior ceilings were high to let the heat rise. Large, magnificent trees were planted to canopy the roof in the summer and let in light during the winter. Think of Tara, the fictional plantation from the movie *Gone with the Wind*, where massive oaks graced the front lawn.

I can remember as a child seeing a huge tree growing next to an old Southern home and wondering why, with all the surrounding land, the tree had to be so close to the house. I now laugh at my naivete. Traditionally, trees were planted for energy conservation. But today trees are planted out front from habit, not necessarily for energy conservation.

This tradition is a good place to go back to, though. If you are going to have trees anyway, why not place them where they can make a difference inside as well?

We seem to have over-engineered our lives in some ways. My house was designed to be air-conditioned. In the mid-south, it would be miserable not to have air conditioning during the summer in our modern homes. It is impractical now to raise the ceilings of my circa-1972, two-story home to let the still summer air rise and settle above our heads.

Large trees like this oak provide shade and cool down the temperature inside the house, saving electricity.

An outdoor hammock is a great place to relax on sunny days—
another benefit of energy-conserving shade trees.

But I can change the landscape to help my home with energy efficiency. Adding shade from trees, shrubs, or vines lowers the amount of heat from the sun's rays (solar radiation) that will reach a home's walls, windows, and roof. In my own home, during the summer months while I waited for my well-placed trees to mature, I pulled the shades on my west-facing side in the afternoons. I could routinely measure a 20-degree difference in the afternoon sun with the shade open versus with the shade closed. Even now that I have mature trees, I pull the shades down in the summer for added benefit.

East- or west-facing windows are particularly bad because they heat up horribly in the summer through solar radiation. South-facing glass is better and can help heat a home in winter. Adding plants around your home will help regulate the sun's effect during different seasons.

Your home's axis is likely different from mine, and it's important to know which direction your home aligns to determine where best to position your plants. Learn to find north, south, east, and west. The best way to do this is to observe east and west during the vernal equinox (late March in the northern hemisphere) or the autumnal equinox (late September). These are the only two days of the year when the sun rises in true east and sets in true west. (The rest of the year, the sun rises and sets generally east and west, respectively.) It's also interesting to watch the changes of the earth's movement around the sun. From the vernal equinox until the summer solstice (the longest day of the year), the sun rises more to the northeast. After the summer equinox and until the vernal equinox, the sun rises more to the southeast.

Create summer shade by locating plants along the sunny borders of the home. Shade south-facing roof and wall surfaces that will receive the most direct sunlight during midday, when the sun is higher in the sky. Also place plants to shade walls that generally face east or west. These walls receive direct sunlight in the morning (for the east) and afternoon (for the west). The eastern morning sun is not as harsh as the western afternoon sun, but keeping the home from heating up too much early in the morning will better control the temperature throughout the day.

By planting deciduous trees in the arc of the sun, you protect the home on the eastern, southeastern, southern, southwestern, and western sides. Carefully select shade trees based on the mature height and structure of the trees so they will be properly spaced and provide the desired shade. A two-story home will need a taller tree than a single-story ranch. The branch structure of a tree makes a difference in its cooling effect in summer and its ability to let in sunshine in winter. Placement of trees will also depend on the shape of the tree crown: V-shaped, pyramidal, round, oval, columnar, and so on. Summer shade for a south-facing roof generally depends on having overhanging tree crowns; without this, shadows will not be cast at midday.

For maximum benefit, it's best to place your plants as close to the home as practical, choosing trees that are not susceptible to disease and breakage. Leaves gathering in the gutters are an unfortunate consequence but consider whether the inconvenience of annual maintenance outweighs the energy conservation benefits that the shade provides.

Choose vines and shrubs in a similar way. Cover walls that face east or west with clumps of vegetation. Use deciduous or evergreen shrubs or small trees that will grow high enough to shade the wall. Vines may be grown directly on masonry walls, but if you have wooden walls, it's better to grow them on a trellis. Otherwise, insects may invade the integrity of your structure.

To learn about the best species of trees, shrubs, or vines for your particular conditions and needs, consult your county extension office.

You don't need to neglect aesthetics in favor of energy conservation. Remember to landscape with your view from the inside in mind, as well as the overall appeal outdoors. Try, for example, sketching potential trees on a photograph, as I suggest in chapter 2 (beginning on page 25). You will quickly begin to see how planting for energy conservation can enhance your home and yard.

The Value of Shade

When we first moved into our home, there were a number of loblolly pine trees throughout the property, particularly in the front. They were tall, some as tall as 80 feet (24.4m). When I looked out the window, all I could see were fat sticks. The only canopy I could see was on the pines across the street.

Lightning started to take a liking to our pines; first one tree was hit, then another. They became a safety hazard. One year, we removed 11 pine trees in our west-facing front yard. The impact of their loss, in terms of heating up the inside of the house in summer, was so noticeable I had to go to work instantly, covering the windows with thick thermal blackout shades. I had no idea the pines had provided so much shade to our home. To me, they just looked like a bunch of sticks. The canopy was too tall to shade the roof, but clearly the thickness of the trees had blocked the harsh summer sun in the afternoons, creating a "moving shade" that was more effective than I thought possible.

To replace them, I added two deciduous trees—one on the left, a coral bark maple (*Acer palmatum* 'Sango kaku'), and one on the right, a crape myrtle (*Lagerstroemia × fauriei* 'Natchez'). Even though they don't provide shade over the roof at noon, they block the afternoon sun from hitting the front wall of the house. They are now mature, and they make it very comfortable inside during the summer, so much so that the air conditioning doesn't have to work as hard.

An excellent reference book on energy efficiency and gardening is *Energy-Wise Landscape Design* by Sue Reed. It is hard to overstate the increase in comfort and benefit to your finances you can achieve with a few careful selections.

CHAPTER 44

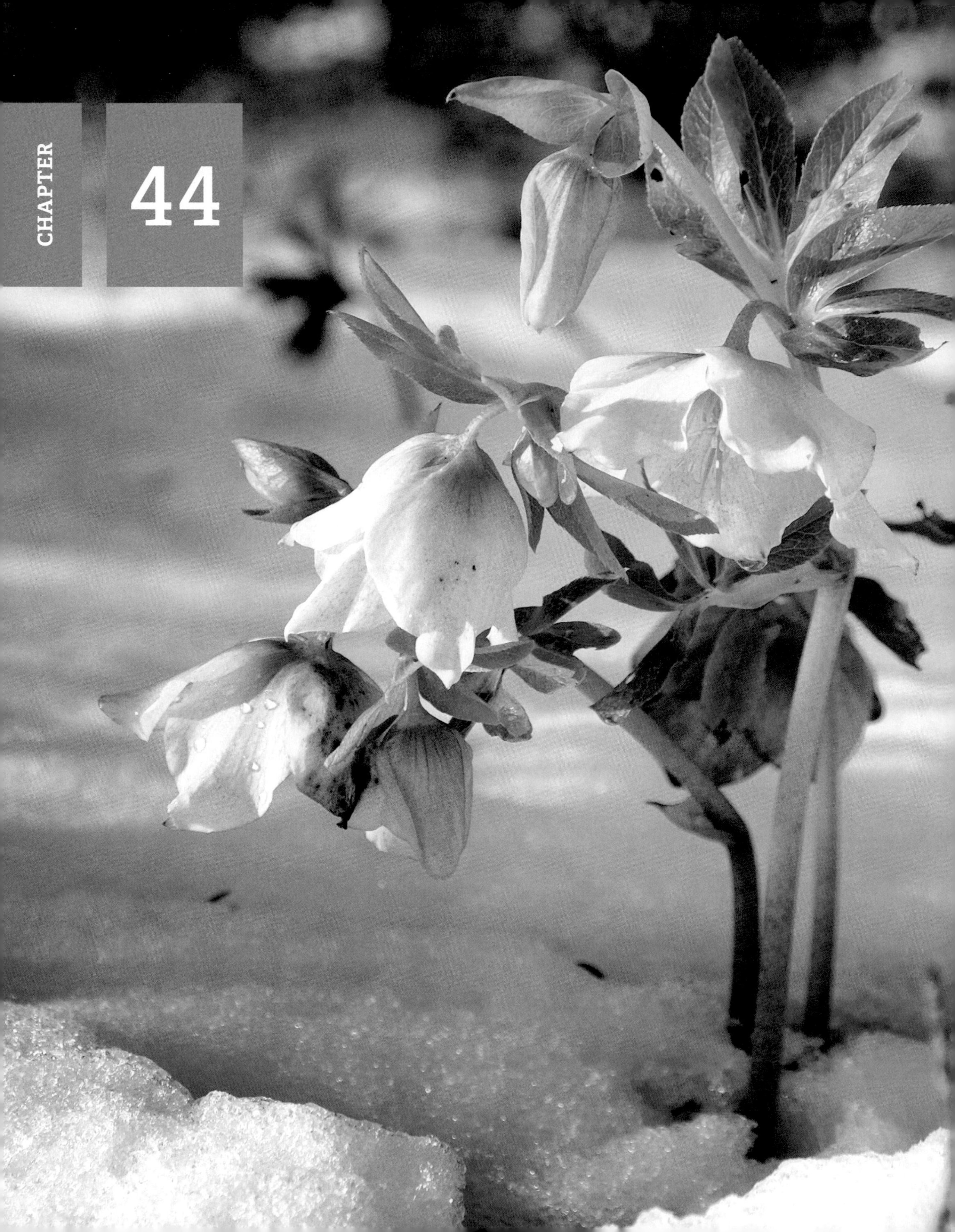

GARDENING FOR THE SEASONS

"Winter is an etching, spring
a watercolor, summer an oil painting,
and autumn a mosaic of them all."
—Stanley Horowitz

Find pleasure in your garden year-round. As you plan and plant your garden, include something of interest for all the seasons. There is beauty in each and every one for you to enjoy.

Winter

If you don't have a garden worthy of winter, you are indeed missing out. No matter if your garden is protected with an insulation of consistent snow cover or warmed with an extra inch of organic mulch, gardening for the winter will bring you great rewards. If done right, you'll find that the berries, bark, wildlife, and even flowers will make you eager to walk in your garden and dream of spring.

In winter, you can focus on admiring the garden space and the visiting wildlife instead of worrying about weeds. While your winter-flowering trees and shrubs are in bloom, the weeds sleep. With the branches of the deciduous trees exposed, the sky is open and brighter, helping to light a gray winter day. The absence of leaves provides the opportunity to really examine a plant— arching, sinuous, textured, or muscular. You will develop a new appreciation for plants and

White hellebores peeking through the snow.

Spring flowers bloom in the garden border.

trees in the landscape when you take the time to study their structures.

Spring

Spring can feel rushed, as if it lasts only days instead of weeks, but there is excitement for the garden season ahead. There is something wonderful in watching as a bare, open sky slowly closes a little each day as trees fill with leaves and shrubs flower. For most of us, spring arrives with the first iconic blossom—a tulip, a daffodil, or a crocus. This experience is further enhanced when the sun breaks through after a cold, rainy day. Just when you don't think you can take another day of winter, a flower reminds you of new life ahead.

Indeed, spring can charm the honey from a bee. Color and kindness abound. The days are ever longer, and the garden is active, urging you to be in the moment. There is an overpowering desire to be with nature.

Each day is a new discovery as you walk through the garden. Spring bulbs planted in the fall will give you instant joy, reminding you that fall efforts bring so many good rewards.

Summer

Summer conjures up thoughts of cookouts, camping, and anything related to water (pools, beaches, lakes, etc.). For many people, gardening is abandoned when spring's door swings shut. For me, however, gardening remains one of my favorite summer pastimes, despite the heat. As a natural early riser, I welcome the morning in the garden. While the temperatures are at their coolest, I can weed, putter, and peek at the flowers.

As the dew dries and the sun rises, the wild creatures wake from restful naps. A butterfly comes out from under a leaf; a frog opens one eye, then the other, with thoughts of breakfast; and a bee asleep on a flower's head won't have far to travel for brunch. There is life in the garden beyond spring. Summer is the time when evenings are spent keeping rhythm with your rocker to the sounds of frogs and crickets serenading you in the waning light. Forget streaming services—cicadas will make your music during the heat of the day, and the bumblebees will hum as they become weighted down with pollen. Planting summer flowers gives your summer garden a voice, so don't let spring be the end of your year in the garden. Plan for summer to hear your garden sing.

Fall

As I journey through my late fall garden, the air is dry, resulting in intense color. Reds are redder, yellows yellower, and late-blooming plants show their brightest and most fragrant blooms in the cooler afternoons. There is still much to enjoy.

Grasses have peaked, providing texture to the landscape, food and hiding places for wildlife, and next year's nesting material. Asters assist the honeybee by providing a protein source, and goldenrod gilds the lily. Why not go out with a colorful, exuberant bang?

Fall gardening does not need to be about only what needs to be done to get ready for winter. It can also be about what is available now. In the wise words of garden writer Elizabeth Lawrence, "Even if something is left undone, everyone must take time to sit still and watch the leaves turn."

Take Joy in Every Season

In Raleigh's mild but four-season Zone 7b climate, it's easy to be a year-round gardener, but surprisingly few are. All seasons aren't created equal—from chores and duties (like planting, pruning, and deadheading) to enjoying the space. Gardening isn't seasonal; it's a state of mind. My garden was built to have no off season. Even in snow cover, the "bones" display formal lines emphasizing the overall design intention. In autumn, fall flowers highlight the garden as a natural wildlife habitat, enticing exuberance. Spring is pure fantasy, with crocuses popping through the lawn and daffodils dancing in just about every section of the garden. Summer, other than deadheading, is about as quiet in my garden as winter.

It's funny how nature regulates us. When the most work needs to be done—spring and fall—the weather is more pleasant for completing those tasks. During the extreme temperatures of summer and winter, we enter a time when we can admire and enjoy the garden while building a list for the upcoming seasons.

CHAPTER 45

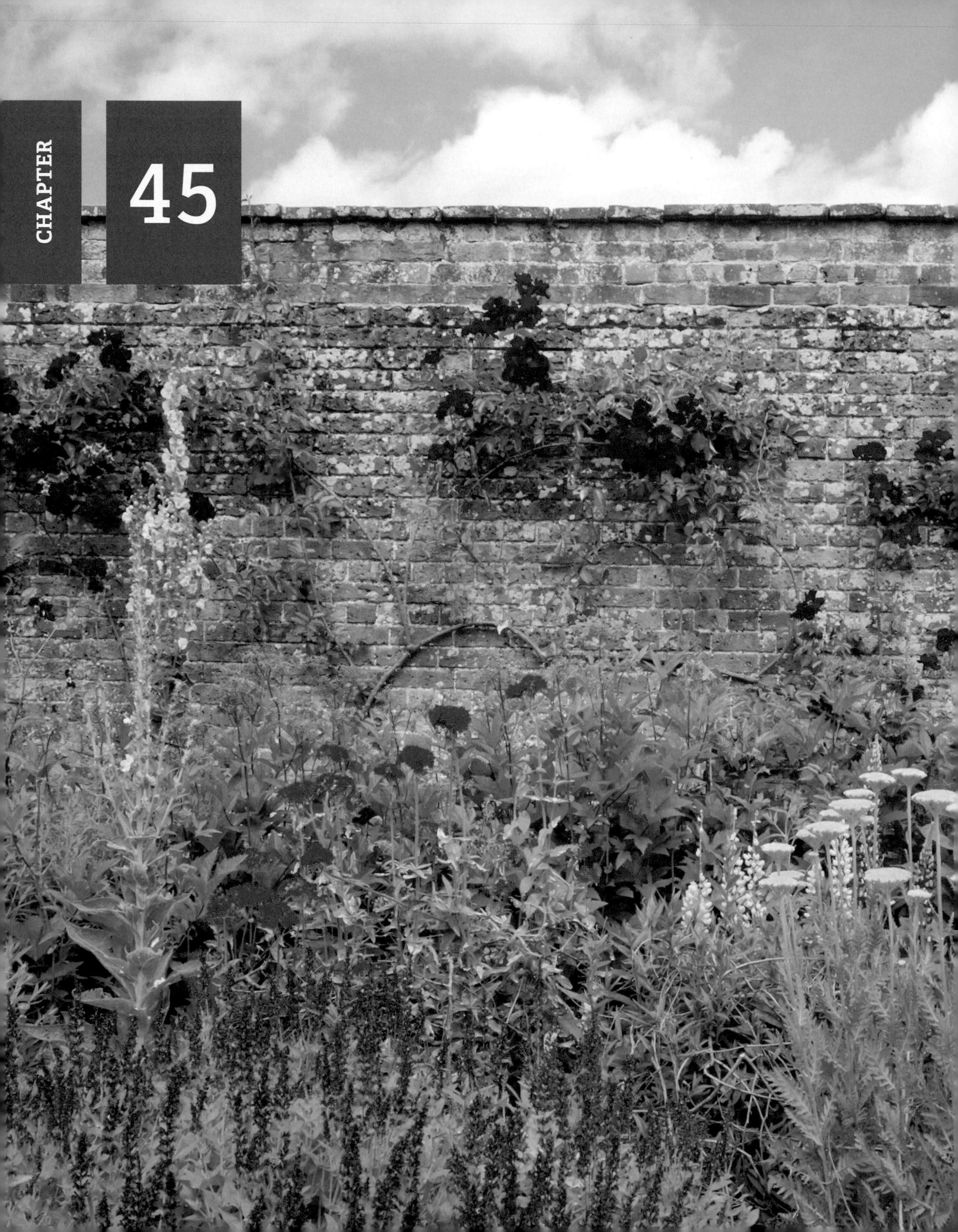

LAYERING THE LANDSCAPE

L ow to the ground or raised high, layers in your landscape give you the opportunity to add more plantings to your garden by taking advantage of each plane level.

The idea of layering dates back to early 20th-century gardens, which were tiered, like a church choir, for better viewing. Gardens following this design have plants arranged in three planes—an upper layer at the back of the border with trees and large shrubs, an intermediate layer containing bold grasses and smaller shrubs, and a lower layer of dwarf shrubs and perennials located at the front border. This stepped arrangement of heights allows every plant to be fully visible and receive optimal exposure from at least one direction. The strategy works best in a deep planting area using a variety of plant heights and situated adjacent to a lawn. For beds dug in the middle of a lawn, the design can be modified by placing the upper layer in the middle of the bed and then stepping down on all sides, creating a pyramid shape.

Today, layering includes those three planes plus two more, what I'm calling the ground and air planes. Adding more layers with ground covers, annuals, and vines gives a more natural feeling and also allows for a greater variety of plants. Here is a quick look at the planes and some plant possibilities for each.

Layers add depth and joy in the country garden.

UPPER PLANE
Small Trees and Large Shrubs

Choose trees for height and large shrubs to balance the height of the trees. These can be evergreen or deciduous, open or tightly branched. They will make up just one plane, but each plant in the plane has equal importance. In my border, I grow native dogwoods and redbuds along with big, large-leafed azaleas.

INTERMEDIATE PLANE
Small Shrubs, Bold Grasses, Perennials, and Annuals

As the name suggests, the intermediate plane is at about half the height of the upper. This is a choice spot for tall perennials such as purple coneflowers (*Echinacea purpurea*) and annuals such as cosmos, which have varieties that grow up to 7 feet (2.1m) tall. Even bulbs can make a welcome addition to the garden—canna, iris, or lilies. Grasses are great here, too, whether big and bold, like common pampas grass, or tender and sweet, like Mexican feathergrass (*Nassella tenuissima*). As with any plant, be sure to check with your county extension agent for information on their invasiveness in your area.

LOWER PLANE
Perennials, Annuals

The lower plane will offer up a huge variety of both annuals and perennials along with dwarf conifers and shrubs. My spring lower plane is filled with native columbine (*Aquilegia*), sedums, coreopsis, and hellebores. Summer sizzles up more sedums, phlox, and some of the more interesting varieties of *Pericaria amplexicaulis*, such as *P. amplexicaulis* 'Firetail'.

GROUND PLANE
Ground Covers

I don't like to see the ground, even though it's covered with a rich, brown mulch made from composted leaves—I would rather see plants. Discovering ground covers has become a great sport for me. I don't seem to tire of them—dwarf mondo grass (*Ophiopogon japonicus*); moss (acrocarps and pleurocarps); sedums; veronicas, such as Georgia blue (*Veronica peduncularis* 'Georgia Blue'); candytufts (*Iberis sempervirens*); and even irises, such as the dwarf crested iris (*Iris cristata*).

AIR PLANE
Climbers and Vines

Designing with vines is a great way to bring your garden to new heights. Vines also add mood to the landscape—mystery, maturity, opulence, abundance, romance, and adventure. Vines can hide an undesirable, such as a drain spout, or can accent a particular area of your home, such as the porch entrance. A home covered in vines is the epitome of idyllic charm. For these and many more reasons, designing with vines adds interest and style to your home.

Vines climb using a variety of means, and it's useful to know how they do so in order to buy the best vine for your purpose. Some vines need more help than others to climb. Vines are grouped either as clingers, twiners, tendrils, or spikers:

- **Clingers**—Using tiny root hairs, clinging vines attach to surfaces. English ivy, creeping fig, and climbing hydrangea are good examples of clinging vines. If you pull the vine off the wall, it leaves marks from where the rootlets were attached. These vines need no support. They freely climb using their own resources.
- **Twiners**—These vines use their stems to twine around a structure, such as a trellis, porch post, gazebo, or arbor. These types of vines include wisteria, morning glory, and hops. They wrap their stems around suitable supports and pull themselves up.
- **Tendrils**—Certain vines use either stem or leaf tendrils like little lassos to climb. Looking closely at the vine, you will see that the tendril will either come from the leaf or the stem to grab whatever is handy to pull itself along. Grapevines, clematis, sweet peas, and passionflowers use tendrils to travel.
- **Spikers**—Spikers spike into something, using their thorns to pull themselves along. Spikers tend to need a little help with support to go where you want them to go. Climbing roses use their thorns to climb. Tying the canes onto a sturdy trellis or wiring them onto a fence at various locations will help your spiker along.

It's also perfectly OK to skip a step along the way so everything doesn't look matchy-matchy. If you follow a formula with tall plants in the back (or middle, depending on the location of the bed) and plant sizes gradually getting shorter toward the front, it can look monotonous. Adding occasional tallish plants in the front will break up the flow and add interest. Tall, wispy plants work best, as the shorter plants will still be visible through them. Airy grasses like lovegrass (*Eragrostis spectabilis*) or spiky plants like verbena on a stick (*Verbena bonariensis*) are good choices.

GARDENING WITH CONFIDENCE

Year-Round Blooms

When I designed my perennial border, I used many English border design principles, including choosing plants to create a layering effect. The English also design to have something in bloom for every month of the growing season. In my case in Raleigh, that's possible to do even in January. Galanthus, crocuses, and certain varieties of daffodils will bloom in January, as will edgeworthia, flowering apricot (*Prunus mume*), witch hazel (*Hamamelidaceae* spp.), and camellias, to name just a few. The red twig dogwood adds color, and the old flower heads of the hydrangea add interest.

To incorporate more blooms in your garden, work with a designer who is plant savvy and can suggest an array of beautiful plantings to give your garden color year-round. Also, as I mentioned earlier (see chapter 31, beginning on page 131), visiting local arboreta, garden centers, and friends' gardens during each season, and in each month, will show you what's blooming when. It's a good opportunity to take notes for future purchases.

IDEAS FOR REDUCING LAWN

My kids rule the turf. Soccer, golf, and football are played on this grass nearly every day. The center turf is also a transitional place when the kids run through the garden with my husband playing freeze tag or other outside chase games. I mow it and it's comforting to me to do so. However, over the years, I've reduced my lawn and added more beds and trees, using ground covers as lawn replacement. The beds are less maintenance than caring for more lawn, and I was able to add plant diversity to provide for the wildlife. I like my lawn for the purpose it serves, but I don't want any more than I need. As the kids grow older, I'll convert more lawn to lower-maintenance options.

Got moss? This earth-hugging, drought-tolerant plant would completely satisfy my need for open, green lushness. I've been experimenting with *Entodon seductrix*, a low-spreading, shiny, multi-branched pleurocarp, making it a worthy lawn replacement. In moist sites, *Entodon seductrix* will form a thick moss mat, with stem branches growing upward from a horizontal main stem—a good moss choice for sunny areas as long as afternoon shade is provided. *Thuidium delicatulum*, which has superior growth and walk-ability, is another option but must also have afternoon shade. For even shadier spots, *Plagiomnium cuspidatum* is a good choice.

In other shady areas where I've reduced lawn while having a bit of change to spare (this is a pricy ground cover option), I grow

Even a small garden space is a nice escape into nature in your own backyard.

Ophiopogon japonicus 'Nana' dwarf mondo grass (Zones 6–9). This finely textured evergreen perennial grows in low, grass-like clumps or mounds in part sun to shade. *Ophiopogon japonicus* is usually a bit taller than the cultivar 'Nana' and is the perfect lawn replacement for those who still want the look of grass.

I've begun to add sun-loving ground covers where turf used to be. As I give my beds a broader berth, I don't worry about scale in terms of what to plant in front of the beds. Instead, I add interesting ground covers that serve as turf replacement, bridging the edge of the grass with the edge of the garden bed. The following are a few of the ground covers I've added to my garden.

In the sunny parts of my Southeast regional garden (Zone 7b), I've incorporated *Rubus calycinoides*, ornamental or creeping raspberry (Zones 6–9), which reaches heights of 6 to 12 inches (15.2 to 30.5cm), and spreads 18 to 24 inches (45.7 to 61cm). Mine grows equally well in sun or shade. Its deep green color, thick texture, and relatively long, spreading branches, make ornamental creeping raspberry an excellent choice as a lawn replacement.

Other sunny bed edges in my yard are swathed with *Dianthus plumarius* (Zones 3–9), which reaches 2 to 5 inches (5.1 to 12.7cm) in height, and spreads 12 to 18 inches (30.5 to 45.7cm). *Dianthus plumarius* are affectionately known as pinks. This common name is not derived from the color of the flowers, since pinks come in colors other than pink, including bicolor. Pinks get their name for the fringed or pinking shear–like edges of the flowers. Pinks also offer another green ground cover choice with a twist, adding a blue-green color to your lawn replacement.

Sedum rupestre 'Angelina', commonly called Angelina stonecrop (Zones 3–11) is gangly, but it still reaches 4 to 6 inches (10.2 to 15.2cm) in height before settling and is a good spreader at 12 to 18 inches (30.5 to 45.7cm) wide. *Sedum rupestre* 'Angelina' makes an unusual ground cover for sunny locations in areas with poor, dry soil. Fleshy, needle-like foliage forms a trailing mat of succulent, star-shaped flowers during the summer months. During the autumn and winter, the foliage often turns amber tones.

Even with the reductions of turf over the years, the kids still have plenty of grassy areas to play their sports. Adding more beds with lawn replacements reduced the amount of time I spent on maintenance—allowing me to pitch a baseball, kick a soccer ball, and generally play outside with the kids a bit more.

This contemporary, urban garden space benefits from a mix of lawn and more unexpected ground covers.

GARDENING WITH CONFIDENCE

Enjoy the Present, Envision the Future

One day my kids will move on, and even then, I'll keep some grass. I do dream, however, of how I will change the wide-open area currently being used as the soccer field. I'm not exactly sure which direction I'll go yet, maybe a parterre (an ornamental garden with paths between the beds), or a rill of water running through the cool, lush grass. My mind wonders if the rill should be a sinuous line, or if it should follow the straight English framework of the existing design. Or should I just plant trees? I envision myself on a hammock, comfortably sipping iced tea. But then I get kicked in the head with a soccer ball, bringing me back into reality where I consider myself very fortunate that I have these three kids to share the great outdoors with just a couple of steps off the back patio.

SIMPLY SUSTAINABLE

The term "sustainable gardening" seems to have become *the* buzzword in the gardening community, encompassing green, organic, and waterwise gardening practices. Simply put, sustainable gardening is the gardening practice of conserving ecological balance by avoiding depletion of natural resources.

Gardening sustainably isn't an all-or-nothing proposition. You can begin with one practice and build from there. What's important is to be aware of what processes you're already using and think about them before you continue with business as usual. It is also good to understand the available options and gradually add more.

Here's a good place to start: Grow the right plants in the right places, and practice water conservation, bed preparation and maintenance, and Integrated Pest Management (IPM).

Proper plant placement will save you time, energy, and resources. Planting moisture-loving plants in a dry bed is counterproductive. Study and know your site; then plant accordingly. While you can often nurse a shade-loving plant in sun with extra water, it's just not sustainable.

Water conservation can be achieved in many aspects of garden design and harvesting. The goal for water conservation is

Sustainable gardening protects our natural resources while we create lovely spaces to enjoy.

to keep as much of the water on your property as possible. This can be done by following these practices:

- Reduce impervious surfaces (hard surfaces that water cannot penetrate).
- Slow falling rainwater enough so it won't go straight into the storm drains.
- Build rain gardens in areas where water collects.
- Use less water—and use it intelligently.

Also, water plants directly at the root zone by hand or using soaker or drip irrigation. Overhead sprinklers are not sustainable, due to the water lost through evaporation and wind. Water according to the plant needs, not a rigid schedule, and water infrequently but deeply.

Everyone's soil is different. It's not uncommon for the soil to change just a few feet away, let alone a few miles away. In my area of the Carolinas, soils range from clay to sand. We can accept our soil and grow plants suitable for that soil type, or we can amend the soil. For any garden soil type, you cannot go wrong in adding more organic matter. In clay soil, organic matter will break up the clay, improving drainage. In sandy soil, organic matter will help retain water.

Covering garden beds with mulch is one of the best things you can do. Used generously, mulch breaks down to add nutrients to the soil, helps retain moisture, moderates the soil temperature, improves soil texture, and suppresses weeds.

Composting garden and kitchen waste is a good sustainable practice. Even if you live in an area with a separate waste pickup that takes yard waste to a composting facility, it's still more sustainable to do your own compost. The less often a yard waste truck has to stop, the more sustainable your efforts will be.

IPM is an effective approach to pest management that uses the most economical means with the least possible hazard to people, property, and the environment. IPM is not a single pest-control method, but rather a series of evaluations, decisions, and controls. It involves the judicious use of pesticides.

IPM follows a four-tiered approach. Seeing a single pest doesn't necessarily mean control is needed. Evaluate each sighting to determine what to do next.

A few well-thought-out practices will easily make your garden more sustainable. Why not start today?

Birds that visit your garden are natural pest controllers, so a birdbath that attracts them is an important part of a sustainable garden.

GARDENING WITH CONFIDENCE

Compost with Style

Even compost piles can be stylish. In my home garden, I compost in a way referred to as a "cold process." That simply means compostable materials are piled up. There is no turning involved. The temperature doesn't rise as high, which slows the process. It works for me, though, because I have two places in my garden where I can compost. While I am using one, the other area is covered. I cover the compost pile with pine straw. Then I let nature do her thing.

Here's another tip: If my garden is scheduled for a garden tour, or if I have a big group stopping by for a visit, or even a few friends over for dinner, I'll top-dress my compost pile just to make things tidy. Otherwise, I see my compost pile as a part of my garden—something to be proud of, not hidden away. And, as an added bonus, having a compost pile makes gardening easier during maintenance and deadheading times.

WATER-WISE GARDENING

There was a time when I thought of water as a renewable resource. Deep down, I still want to believe this. Although our water supply does get recharged (some years are better than others), the distribution of this water over my lot and over my garden varies. Each year, the gain isn't necessarily equal to the loss—sometimes we take more than nature gives.

Since I come from a land of 44 inches (1.1m) of rain a year, you may be surprised to hear me touting water-wise garden design. Out in the West, this is a way of life. However, on the East Coast, we still experience long periods of drought. If Raleigh's annual rainfall came an inch a week, there would be little need for a water-wise design. But it doesn't. Summers, in particular, can be hot and dry. It wasn't until we were experiencing the worst drought in 100 years, with outdoor watering restrictions and no major rain in sight, that I began to take note.

Water-wise gardening is not new, but gardeners seem to have drifted from understanding the benefits and techniques of water-wise design. This strategy is not limited to gardening in a drought, it is also a practical and effective way to garden anywhere, while at the same time promoting good environmental stewardship of our land and water.

The main way to achieve a water-wise design is to group plants with similar needs together. My design has saved me countless hours of watering, plus the cost associated with that. But I soon realized a water-saving

A xeriscape garden (one developed especially for arid or semiarid climates) featuring water-wise plants.

design also cemented a map of my garden and thereby simplified my plant purchases.

In the past, before acquiring a plant, I would only think of the plant's sun requirements. If it needed extra water and I loved the plant, I didn't pay much attention to where I planted it. I assumed that I would stay on top of its needs. I rarely did, of course. Now when I select a plant, I think of not only the sun requirements, but water requirements, as well. I know exactly where in my garden the plant can go, based on the map of my water-wise garden. Today, I'll put a plant back on the shelf if I can't meet its sun requirements and also find room in the appropriate bed. Although it was hard at first, looking back, I have no regrets. With so many great plants out there, I'll just keep looking for those that meet my needs.

Remember, too, water-wise isn't limited to drought-tolerant plants. It's a planting scheme that uses all different kinds of plants, from agaves to tropicals, and groups them in efficient beds based on their various watering needs. The beds in a water-wise garden are divided into three gardening zones: oasis, transitional, and xeric.

- The **oasis zone** is the area closest to the water source. These sources can be rainspouts, rain barrels, or a faucet and hose. Also include the area around the front door as an oasis, where you can easily water container plants with water collected indoors.
- The **transitional zone** is the area away from the house, about midway from the home to the end of the property. Plantings here should be sustainable, requiring only

Water-conscious gardening still leads to healthy plants.

GARDENING WITH CONFIDENCE

The Water-Wise Approach to Fountains

Being water-wise goes beyond plant choices and bed placements. Think about other garden features, as well. A major focal point in my front garden is a 6-foot-tall (1.8m-tall), three-tiered fountain. It is a fantastic feature for creating sound, attracting wildlife, and adding beauty. I refill the water with harvested rain I capture in a 250-gallon converted food-storage container. These containers abound since they have only a one-time use. After their initial use, they either go to the landfill or clever people find ways to repurpose them. They make great rain harvesters for gardeners, and only slight modifications are needed. My harvester sits at the corner of the property on the south side—the same side the fountain is on—but the harvester is next to the house. The drain spout diverts rainwater into the harvester, with overflow going to an oasis bed. I have a hose hooked up at the bottom of the harvester. When the fountain needs refilling, all I need to do is turn the valve. If I don't have water, I don't turn on the fountain. It still provides water for the wildlife when it's not running. When the fountain is running, it's a signal to all that we are rain rich (for the moment anyway). While I enjoy the fountain most when it's running, I also value its silence, which means water is being conserved and used only when available. Silence makes a major statement in my garden and in water-wise design.

occasional supplemental water. Typically, these areas are island beds, driveway beds, or raised beds.
- The **xeric zone** is at the property's perimeter. These plants should be tough and should not require supplemental water. This area can be filled with dependable, drought-resistant plants.

It's not difficult to be water-wise. Get a rain gauge and pay attention to the local rainfall. Only water when your plants need watering. Even the thirstiest of plants, once established, only need about an inch of water a week. (However, container gardens may need daily watering in the heat of the summer.) Also, remember to mulch—its moisture-trapping ability will be your best defense against drought!

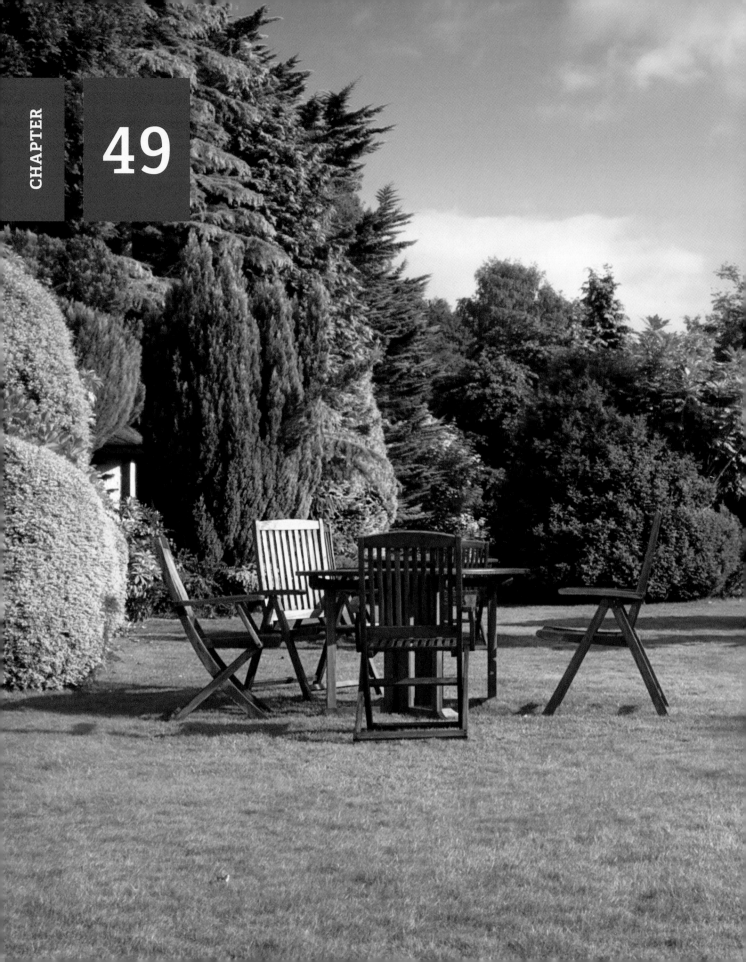

TIME

Try as I might to speed the garden's growth, I've faced the fact that all I really need is patience. As I look around my garden, evaluating what she needs to shine for upcoming garden tours and photo shoots, I realize she just needs time. This is true for most gardens. I don't need to add a little something here or there. The design is set. I just need to wait it out.

This is the hardest part.

Nothing I do now will fill the gaps between the sedum, providing a full tapestry of ground cover under individual specimen plants in the red bed.

Nothing I do now will make the boxwood fill in. My imagination sees a continuous line of boxwood, serving as the transition between formal and casual—the boundary demarcating tameness and wildness.

Nothing I do now will leap the rose of Sharon into adulthood.

Nothing I do now will mature a tree, providing a canopy for shady rest.

What I can do has been done. Now, all I really need is time.

By many standards, my garden is full, lush, and mature. It is only I who see the holes, flaws, and flubs. It's not a garden for everyone and no doubt when people visit for the first time, "high maintenance" might come to mind. I can honestly say it's not a high-maintenance garden, however.

Herein lies the problem. I *like* to putter in my garden. When I run out of things to do, I start tinkering. My thinking is that if I add more, it will serve as a stopgap, a filler until the garden matures.

A full, mature garden requires a bit of patience.

This tinkering must stop. All that my garden needs now is time.

Don't be mistaken; there are many areas for improvement. And, of course, there is the regular maintenance—deadheading, dividing, and pruning. I also need to edit out some of my earlier tinkering. But, for the most part, my garden is not difficult to keep up, and this is something I will appreciate more and more each year.

Oftentimes, I wonder how I would have designed my garden if the children had not been part of the equation or if I had unlimited funds. I begin to dream of a new garden instead of waiting for my existing garden to mature.

Then reality hits, and I realize *this* is my garden for here and now—and for ten or more years from now. At the end of the day, this is the garden for me. For her to flourish, all she needs is time.

If I had it to do over again, I would embrace time more fully. I would let time fill in the gaps, rather than planting closer or adding more to force the mature look. In many ways, I interfered with my garden's natural processes. It was fun, and editing gardens is something I enjoy doing, but the big investments, like trees, could have been better planned. Fortunately, no major mistakes were made. I was able to move ornamental, low-growing trees that were planted too

The reward of a completed garden in full bloom.

close together to give them appropriate space. But it was work that did not need to be done, had I only respected time.

On a side note, letting time nurture your garden does not rule out the possibility of modifying it. Tastes change. Ability changes. So, plant for the future. Get the anchor pieces in place, and you and your garden will be able to handle alterations much more easily.

As I wait for my garden to mature, I'll rest in the comfort that weeds defy time, as do the shrubs that need pruning and the grass that needs mowing. There is always something to be done. But for now, I'm done trying to fix what only time can mature.

GARDENING WITH CONFIDENCE

Splurge Where It Counts

A watched pot never boils, and adding salt to the water doesn't make it boil faster either. But many still do it.

I clearly remember one very hot summer day sitting on my back deck in my old neighborhood, staring at the garden. I was on the edge of my seat with my torso stretched forward, leaning against the railing. My arms were folded in such a way, resting along the top of the railing, that they looked like chicken wings.

I had just spent the entire day adding a hedgerow of conifers for privacy on the perimeter of a neighboring property when another neighbor called out, "Whatcha doing, Helen? Watching the grass grow?" He was almost right. I was watching the one-gallon plants I had just put into the ground, trying to visualize what they would look like mature and topping 15 feet (4.6m). The next day I watched them, then the next, and the next. Each day for the rest of our time there, I checked the height of those shrubs. We didn't live there long enough for me to see them mature.

There are some plants that you should splurge on. Instead of buying one-gallon plants, buy three- or seven-gallon pots or even ball and burlap, if need be.

When we left that garden for the home we're in now, I did just that. I jump-started the garden by using taller plants, so I didn't have to obsess over watching the shrubs grow. If you found me staring, I was not wishing for something I didn't have any control over—it was just pure admiration. Today, our garden has a mature hedgerow providing privacy in our back garden and also serving as a backdrop for various other plantings. Especially when it comes to privacy, do yourself a favor, and buy bigger. You won't regret it.

CHAPTER

50

Working with the plants and styles you love most will boost your confidence in the garden.

GARDENING WITH CONFIDENCE

Learn from Mistakes

There was the time I planted seven gorgeous hostas in a new bed only to wake up and find them nearly gone. Every one was chomped off at the root level, and most of the foliage was dragged down under the ground and finished off.

It was voles! Voles are herbivores, and they find the roots of hostas, camellias, roses, and *Aspidistra elatior* (cast-iron plant) much to their liking.

Would you believe I replanted? I did some research and followed some very sound advice. As advised, I planted with the hosta still in the pot, wrapped in landscape fabric around the top, sides, and drainage hole. For good measure, I heavily sprinkled the area with PermaTill®, a soil conditioner. I planted my seven new hostas—but when I checked on them the next morning, they were gone.

Now I was out of time, patience, and money. I gave up and planted hellebores instead and haven't had a problem since. Voles don't like hellebores.

I wasn't so lucky the time the voles went after my *Aspidistra elatior*. Thank goodness these cast-iron plants were only a rather pedestrian solid-green variety. I planted five one day, and as is my habit, I went to check on them the next day. Three were gone. I was outraged. I knew there were voles in this area, but I didn't know voles liked cast-iron plants. So, what did I do? I did something that puts me into the "don't that beat all!" category. I moved the remaining two cast-iron plants to a new location where I knew there were no voles. The next morning when I went to check on these two plants, they were down on the ground.

There was only one explanation: I must have transplanted a vole with a plant. If this ever happens to you, you have two choices—laugh or cry.

I chose to laugh and continue gardening with confidence because, hey, life happens. Never give up. Note the lesson and start again.

GARDENING WITH CONFIDENCE

When you first read the name of this chapter, you might think it a bit cocky. It's not meant to be. This idea was given to me by my husband, David, as he watched me work in the garden. He said, "You really know how to garden with confidence." He told me that I make it look so easy—he was always my biggest fan.

But I didn't always garden with confidence. At first, I was driven by the desire to really know how to garden, not just to be schooled in design or plant culture or pruning basics. I wanted to understand what it is to garden, but I worried too much whether I was doing it "right."

After a while, I learned there isn't really a whole lot I can mess up. If you alleviate this fear of messing up with a little logic and forethought, you can avoid making even the few possible major mistakes.

Confidence is built by using the right tools, preparing for the elements, and visiting other gardens and local arboreta in your area for ideas on what grows well in your area. Meeting other gardeners, talking with the staff at your independent garden center, reading regional blogs, and even chatting on garden forums will do even more to boost your confidence. But most importantly, confidence comes from faith in yourself to get out and dig.

The gardening community is vast. Every town has a "go-to" person, or several people, for various interests. Search for any gardening topic on the internet, and you'll find a hundred or more sources. Go to plant sales, join a garden club, and listen to lectures. And don't be afraid to ask questions. I'd bet I ask at least one garden-related question a day of people who know the things I want to learn. I know what I know, and I know what I don't know.

Sometimes I learn something that I didn't even know I should know. Those are the best days. Somewhere along the way, I got so much confidence that I was comfortable enough to say, "I don't know the answer to that, but I'm happy to look into it." And that was when I really began to learn.

When you meet me, you'll find I have the annoying little habit of picking your brain to learn what you know or how you go about doing a certain task. My world is wide open to learning new ways to benchmark, become better, or do something with greater ease. If I meet a plant propagator, I don't bother asking what their favorite flower is or for tips to amend the soil. Instead, I pull a question from my memory bank and ask about when and how to propagate a particular plant I'm interested in learning about.

Never be afraid of admitting what you don't know. Be assured that there are no stupid questions. This is the secret to gardening with confidence. Gardeners are always at the ready to share information.

From the time I started gardening as a child with my dad showing me the way—and me, no doubt, annoying him with all my questions—to today, when I am asking you questions and looking for what you can teach me, I am learning to garden with confidence. I know that I can only mess up just so badly. And, oh yes, plants have died, but I didn't necessarily kill them.

Gardeners like you make the best resources. It's better still when you put your guard down to teach me or show me or tell what you think about this or that. In this way, you will gain a little bit more confidence, too.

I hope this book helped you gain confidence and garner a new perspective for viewing various gardening styles and elements. Since 1997, I've gardened with confidence on a half-acre wildlife habitat on a suburban lot in Raleigh, North Carolina—my own garden haven.

INDEX

ACKNOWLEDGMENTS

With the richness I've received from the encouragement to write this book, I could fly to the moon. The Raleigh gardening community and my gardening friends all over the United States have been incredibly supportive of my efforts.

The book idea was formulated following the funeral of my mother in December 2010. My family and I went back to my brother's home in Washington, D.C., for some good conversation and to let the kids burn off some of their energy before we headed back to Raleigh.

As I chatted with my sister-in-law, Charmaine Yoest, giving her an update on my book idea, she said I was writing the exact book she, as a beginner gardener, needed. She wanted not so much a how-to, but more of a why-to and a where-to. She wanted a conversation with a designer to understand how a garden can be built over time as energy and resources become available. For the periods when she wasn't building her garden, she wanted to be able to read about gardening elements, where and how to think about building a garden. Charmaine, I hope I've met your need. I believe you are not alone in wanting such a conversation.

As the book evolved and chapters were written, I sought learned friends to read selected chapters, including Roy C. Dicks, Suzanne Edney, Brent and Becky Heath, Beth Jimenez, Kelly Senser, David Spain, and Bobby J. Ward, as well as Chris Glenn, Barbara Pintozzi, and Christopher Tidrick, who did the final cover-to-cover readings.

Special thanks to Vivian Finkelstein for keeping her laughter to a low roar when I would make a few (well, maybe more than a few) silly grammatical errors and to John Buettner for keeping me laughing as he taught me all I needed to know about a book layout. Also, thanks to Amanda Willms for her copy-editing skills. Mandy, I wish I knew half of what you know. Your talent amazes me; I put it right up there with rocket science. I'm also forever grateful for the gentle hands of Mary Helen Clarke, who formatted my content, and for Gail Eichelberger, who introduced us.

None of this would have been possible, however, without the support of my three wonderful kids and super supportive husband, who unconditionally believes in me and who once said of me changing careers, "You didn't divert from engineering to horticulture, but rather you diverted into engineering from a delayed career in horticulture."

ABOUT THE AUTHOR

Helen Yoest is a lifelong outdoor enthusiast who would much rather spend a day in a garden than anywhere indoors.

Helen was born in Chincoteague, Virginia, and was raised in Norfolk, Virginia. She earned an undergraduate degree from Old Dominion University and a graduate degree in environmental engineering and science from Brunel University in London, England. She spent 20 years as an air pollution field engineer before changing careers to hang her shingle in horticulture. Helen is an honorary member of Pi Alpha Xi, the national horticultural honor society.

Helen is a garden stylist and writer, having penned the books *Good Berry Bad Berry: Who's Edible, Who's Toxic, and How to Tell the Difference (Good . . . Bad)* and *Plants with Benefits: An Uninhibited Guide to the Aphrodisiac Herbs, Fruits, Flowers & Veggies in Your Garden*.

For 15 years, Helen scouted, produced, and wrote for most national gardening magazines, such as *Better Homes and Gardens*, *Country Gardens*, *Southern Living*, and many state and regional titles. Helen was also a writer for *Martha Stewart Living*, *The Christian Science Monitor*, and *Fine Gardening*, along with writing pieces for P. Allen Smith and many others.

Helen served for five years as the regional representative for the Raleigh-area Garden Conservancy's Open Days tour, and is a former member of the board of advisors for the JC Raulston Arboretum and currently advises the Raleigh City Farm.

Helen lives with her husband and three kids in Raleigh, North Carolina.